DATE DUE

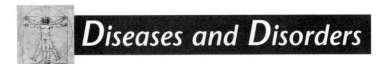

Diseases and Disorders

Phobias

Titles in the Diseases and Disorders series include:

Diseases and Disorders

Phobias

by Gail B. Stewart

Library of Congress Cataloging-in-Publication Data

Stewart, Gail B., 1949–
  Phobias / by Gail B. Stewart.
    p. cm. — (Diseases and disorders series)
  Includes bibliographical references and index.
  Summary: Discusses phobias including: history and research, social and specific phobias, simple phobias, panic attacks and agoraphobia, and overcoming phobias.
    ISBN 1-56006-726-8 (lib. bdg. : alk. paper)
  1. Phobias—Juvenile literature. [1. Phobias.] I. Title. II. Series.
RC535 .S746 2001
616.8'225—dc21   00-010223
                                                       CIP

Copyright © 2001 by Lucent Books, Inc.
P.O. Box 289011
San Diego, CA 92198-9011
Printed in the U.S.A.

Table **of Contents**

"The Most Difficult Puzzles Ever Devised"

CHARLES BEST, ONE of the pioneers in the search for a cure for diabetes, once explained what it is about medical research that intrigued him so. "It's not just the gratification of knowing one is helping people," he confided, "although that probably is a more heroic and selfless motivation. Those feelings may enter in, but truly, what I find best is the feeling of going toe to toe with nature, of trying to solve the most difficult puzzles ever devised. The answers are there somewhere, those keys that will solve the puzzle and make the patient well. But how will those keys be found?"

Since the dawn of civilization, nothing has so puzzled people—and often frightened them, as well—as the onset of illness in a body or mind that had seemed healthy before. A seizure, the inability of a heart to pump, the sudden deterioration of muscle tone in a small child—being unable to reverse such conditions or even to understand why they occur was unspeakably frustrating to healers. Even before there were names for such conditions, even before they were understood at all, each was a reminder of how complex the human body was, and how vulnerable.

While our grappling with understanding diseases has been frustrating at times, it has also provided some of humankind's most heroic accomplishments. Alexander Fleming's accidental discovery in 1928 of a mold that could be turned into penicillin has resulted in the saving of untold millions of lives. The isolation of the enzyme insulin has reversed what was once a death sentence for anyone with diabetes. There have been great strides in combating conditions for which there is not yet a cure, too. Medicines can help AIDS patients live longer, diagnostic tools such as mammography and ultrasounds can help doctors find tumors while they are treatable, and laser surgery techniques have made the most intricate, minute operations routine.

This "toe-to-toe" competition with diseases and disorders is even more remarkable when seen in a historical continuum. An astonishing amount of progress has been made in a very short time. Just two hundred years ago, the existence of germs as a cause of some diseases was unknown. In fact, it was less than 150 years ago that a British surgeon named Joseph Lister had difficulty persuading his fellow doctors that washing their hands before delivering a baby might increase the chances of a healthy delivery (especially if they had just attended to a diseased patient)!

Each book in Lucent's *Diseases and Disorders* series explores a disease or disorder and the knowledge that has been accumulated (or discarded) by doctors through the years. Each book also examines the tools used for pinpointing a diagnosis, as well as the various means that are used to treat or cure a disease. Finally, new ideas are presented—techniques or medicines that may be on the horizon.

Frustration and disappointment are still part of medicine, for not every disease or condition can be cured or prevented. But the limitations of knowledge are being pushed outward constantly; the "most difficult puzzles ever devised" are finding challengers every day.

The Most Dreadful Feeling

WHEN SHERRI VISITS a friend's house, the first question she asks is "Do you have a cat?" Others assume she has allergies and is therefore anxious to avoid the sneezing and watery eyes typical in an allergic reaction to cats. But her problem isn't an allergy, the twenty-two-year-old college student says with a rueful smile.

"I'm petrified of cats," she says. "Simply terrified of them. I don't know why—I never was attacked by a cat or anything. The rest of my family has no problem with cats, so I don't think I was influenced by them at all.

"I started being afraid when I was about twelve, at a friend's house. She had a calico cat that never bothered me before, but all of a sudden when it walked in the room where we were sitting, I panicked! I just lost it—my heart was pounding and I was sweating. I thought I was going to faint. All I could think about was getting out of there as fast as I could. Like my life depended on it.

"It's gotten worse ever since then. I get panicky seeing cats on television, or even a picture of a cat. I won't go anywhere where I know there will be a cat. I even missed a party at my academic adviser's house because his family had just gotten a new kitten. I know it makes no sense to feel this way," says Sherri, "but I can't help it."[1]

"You Just Can't Explain It"

Greg, a thirty-one-year-old computer analyst, wholeheartedly agrees that such fears are senseless, but like Sherri, he has had no luck ridding himself of one. Rather than fear of an animal, however, Greg has suffered with a paralyzing fear of attending any social function, such as a party or a dinner.

"I'm OK with a good friend usually," he says. "But going out with a bunch of people to a bar or a restaurant or something is totally out. I used to like going places, being with people. But now I get scared. I feel like I'm going to do something really stupid, and I'll get looked at, or people will laugh at me."

Greg realizes how foolish his fears are; however, that doesn't make it any easier for him to socialize.

"That's the thing that nobody understands," he explains. "I realize how stupid it sounds, too. And it's had really inconvenient effects on me—I avoid any situation that involves strangers in groups. I don't go out to eat, except takeout. I know I'm missing out on a lot of things that other people think are fun. But unless you have the same fear, you just can't explain it."[2]

More Than Just Being Afraid

The emotion felt by Greg and Sherri is more than simply being afraid of something, say psychologists. Each of them suffers from a phobia, an often paralyzing fear of an object or situation—a fear that is unreasonable considering the object or situation. For instance, even though Sherri is not in any danger of being injured by a kitten or by a picture of a cat, her terrified response to either of these (in addition to her diligence in making sure she never comes in contact with a cat) shows that she has a phobia.

Being frightened of going to a party or of a harmless kitten may seem silly or strange to someone who has never had a phobia. However, phobias are no laughing matter to those who suffer from them. Affecting more than 26 million people, phobias are the number one mental health disorder in the United States—far ahead of depression and substance abuse.

And though it is possible for a person like Sherri to live a fairly normal life simply by avoiding places with cats, many people with phobias are unable to function. An international business executive who is afraid to fly, for example, or a teacher who develops a phobia of talking in front of people can quickly be without a job.

Twenty-six million Americans experience the paralyzing fear that comes with a phobia.

One twenty-two-year-old actor who recently developed a phobia of driving says that it has ruined what he thought would be a great career. "I live in Los Angeles," he says. "It's not exactly the mass-transportation capital of the world, you know? You have no choice in this town other than driving.

"But I've been terrified of driving—even *riding* in cars—for over a year. So I haven't been able to go to auditions, haven't been able to pick up a part-time job to tide me over until I get something. It isn't an exaggeration to say that my phobia has wrecked my life."[3]

Jerilyn Ross, president of the Phobia Society of America, agrees that phobias can—and do—destroy people's aspirations. Says Ross, "There are millions of Americans whose jobs and careers are affected every day by their phobias."[4]

The Toll of Fears

The loss of a career is not the worst price a person with a phobia pays. There is a great deal of emotional and physical stress—often because the phobic person is unaware of the cause of the fear.

"I thought, 'Am I crazy?' or 'Am I having a nervous breakdown?'" one woman recalls. "I was spending hours of time on the phone to nurses' hot lines, to clinics. I didn't want to go to actually see a doctor, because I was afraid he'd say I was insane. I was embarrassed and a little ashamed—I thought, 'How come I'm so panicky?' Nothing I could do seemed to help, and I felt so hopeless."[5]

Because of these feelings of hopelessness, people with acute phobias tend to suffer from clinical depression more often than the general population. They are 50 percent more likely to abuse alcohol and other mood-altering drugs, say psychologists, and are also more prone to suicidal thoughts.

A Good First Step

However, the disruption of a person's social life, career, and health can be reversed. There is a growing body of information about phobias and the panic they cause. Doctors are confident that, in most cases, phobias can be successfully treated. The roadblock to such treatment, they say, is the lack of knowledge about phobias.

Feeling as though their experiences make them "crazy" or "weird," many people with phobias assume that there is no help available or that they are beyond help. "Most people with phobias don't understand their disorder," says one researcher. "They consider themselves weak for letting something like this interfere with their life."[6]

Taking the time to learn about what phobias really are, as well as understanding the physical and mental effects of anxiety and fear, is an important first step for a person with a phobia. The more people know, the more effectively they can begin to deal with the terror they are experiencing.

Chapter 1

Fear and Phobia

PSYCHOLOGISTS AND DOCTORS use terms such as *fear* and *anxiety* when talking about phobias. To understand the nature of phobias—as well as the scope of the difficulties phobias cause for people—it is important to understand what it really means to be anxious and afraid, and what physical and psychological effects these emotions produce.

Two Aspects of Fear

Fear and anxiety are very similar; both emotions produce effects that are far from pleasant. Anxiety is fear at its most vague—an uneasy sense of dread or foreboding about some future event. It is often associated with a tight feeling in the chest and a nervous uncertainty or a feeling of apprehension. One person who is anxious might describe her emotion as a tenseness or uneasiness, and might complain about a tight feeling in her chest. Another might note that his mouth feels dry and he has a queasy, unsettled feeling in his stomach.

Fear, on the other hand, is generally defined as a response to a real (or believed to be real) threat and is therefore more specific than anxiety. People feel fear not about some frightening thing that may confront them in the future but about a threatening thing or event in the here and now. A mail carrier might feel fear at the sight of a snarling dog nearby; a child might feel fear while riding on a roller coaster at the fair.

The feeling of fear is similar to that of anxiety, except more acute. One of the first attempts to clinically describe some of the physical effects of fear was done in the early seventeenth century by clergyman and writer Robert Burton. In his treatise called *The Anatomy of Melancholy*, Burton explains that fear causes "many lamentable effects . . . [such as] to be pale, tremble, sweat; it makes sudden cold and heat to come all over the body, palpitations of the heart, fainting."[7]

A Crucial Response

Because trembling, sweating, and a pounding heart are very uncomfortable physical symptoms, it is understandable why some might dismiss fear as a useless, negative emotion. However, say experts, nothing could be further from the truth. Fear is one of the most important human responses. States psychiatrist Isaac Marks, "Fear is a vital evolutionary legacy. . . . Without fear, few would survive long under natural conditions."[8]

Fear is a primitive survival response, one that has been evolving since our prehistoric ancestors (and other parts of the animal kingdom before them, according to evolutionists). Hundreds of thousands of years ago, fear was critical in keeping people safe from saber-toothed tigers, electrical storms, and other frightening aspects of their world.

In what scientists today call the "fight or flight response," these people would deal with danger either by violently struggling with it (fighting) or by running away from it as quickly as possible (flight). To prepare them for either fight or flight, their bodies would respond with a remarkable series of changes. Vision would become clearer, the heart would pump blood faster, the lungs would work harder to provide an increase in oxygen to the muscles in the legs and arms. Even sweating would notably increase; the body's extra activity would heat it quickly, and the sweat would act as a coolant.

Remnants of the Past

Even though the kinds of dangers or emergencies faced in modern society are usually of a different nature than those of our prehistoric ancestors, those same physical reactions still occur. That's because fear begins deep in the brain, where involuntary, instinctive knowledge is hidden—the same instinctive knowledge that served our prehistoric forebears so well.

Fear expert Donald Goodwin explains that, although a modern response to danger may begin in the more advanced outer part of the brain—the cortex—most of what follows has nothing to do with intellect:

> When you hear the word "Fire!" in a theatre, it is registered in the cortex. But then the "old brain" takes over—the reptilian brain submerged deep beneath the clever new cortex. The old brain does not "study the situation": it acts, and acts the way it has for millions of years in thousands of species going back at least to the earliest vertebrates. It prepares the body to defend itself.[9]

Messages are fired off to the nervous system; in an emergency, it is the sympathetic nervous system (SNS) that responds. The SNS sees that a hormone called adrenaline is released into the bloodstream. It is adrenaline that increases the blood pressure and heart rate for the duration of the emergency. Other parts of the nervous system make sure that muscles along the skeletal system are tensed and ready, either to fight or flee.

The physical effects of fear are noticeable on the outside, too. The eyes of a person who is very frightened will appear very dark, because his pupils become dilated. This response allows every possible bit of light in, to sharpen his vision. A frightened person will also often appear very pale, because a great deal of blood that normally gives the skin a healthy glow is rerouted to the muscles for added strength.

Perhaps the most unusual physical response to fear is that of the body hair, which stands on end when a person is badly frightened. Interestingly, this phenomenon has nothing at all to do with a person's need to flee or fight. In fact, the response was probably just as useless in ancient times as it is today.

Natural historians and scientists explain that hair standing on end is probably the most primitive fear response, and is evidence of humankind's evolution from other mammals. Cats, for example, exhibit this trait when frightened; when their hair stands on end, it makes them appear larger and more frightening to a predator.

In 1872, Charles Darwin, the most famous proponent of the idea of evolution, marveled at how similar fear is exhibited in the animal kingdom:

The primitive fear response that leads to a person's body hair standing on end is most often observed in the domestic cat.

The involuntary bristling of the hair (in animals) serves, together with certain involuntary movements, to make them appear terrible to their enemies. . . . The minute unstriped muscles, by which the hairs thinly scattered over man's almost naked body are erected, still contract under the same emotions, namely terror and rage, which cause the hairs to stand on end in the lower members of the Order to which man belongs.[10]

Making Quick Decisions

To have so much adrenaline in one's system, to have systems of muscles and blood and oxygen operating at such a high level at the very moment that fear strikes, can still be extremely useful, even though the physical dangers are far fewer in modern society. For example, the fear someone feels during a natural disaster such as a storm or flood can help her take immediate action to get to safety.

One woman whose house was literally torn apart by a tornado in 1998 says that she never knew she could move as quickly as she did that afternoon. If she hadn't, she and her ten-month-old son would surely have lost their lives.

"I'd never really understood what people meant about adrenaline," she says. "Now I realize how amazing it is—how your brain and everything can just go on automatic pilot. I think that's the best way to describe it. I don't even remember how I knew to do what I did. I just grabbed my baby and ran down into the basement. I didn't think, I didn't stop to consider all the options. I heard that freight train sound, the horrible sound the wind was making, and I just ran." [11]

"I Felt As Though I'd Run Ten Miles"

Even in situations in which neither fighting nor fleeing would be appropriate, the "fight or flight" sensation is just as strong. One woman named Susan recalls the fear she felt when she heard that her young daughter Lucy had been taken to the hospital after being hit by a car.

"I was the classic subject of fear, the textbook example of 'fight or flight' you study in psychology class," she says. "My heart was pounding so loud I could hear it, my palms were sweaty, and I was very pale—I looked like I'd crawled out from under a rock. My muscles were so tense that I was literally *bouncing* on the balls of my feet. Even my jaw muscles were working overtime—I couldn't stop chattering my teeth. I'd never been that frightened in my whole life, and I hope I never feel it again. It was a horrible feeling.

"All I could think about in the emergency waiting room was whether Lucy was alive. I was a bundle of energy with no place to spend it. I wasn't going to fight anybody, or take flight. But I had all those feelings! Afterwards, more than an hour later when I found out she would live, the fear just kind of seeped away. But that night, I was more tired than I'd ever been in my whole life. Honestly, I felt as though I'd run ten miles." [12]

How Do We Know What to Fear?

Although the strong physical reactions to fear are instinctive, it is not as clear where the fears themselves come from. Why we fear what we do has long been a topic of interest to psychologists and others who study human behavior.

It is known, for example, that some fears are learned. A child who is separated from her parents in a busy shopping mall for a few minutes may be so terrified that she'll be reluctant to let them out of her sight for weeks afterward. If she looks around and doesn't see her mother nearby, she would probably exhibit the fear symptoms described earlier—the pounding heart, the rapid breathing, and so on.

Tim, sixteen, agrees that bad experiences can "teach" one to be afraid. He can remember the exact day that he developed a fear of large dogs.

"It was my fourth birthday, May 28, and I'd had some neighbor friends over for a party. I was walking outside with my friend to try out a toy truck I got when it happened. I had the truck in one hand and a piece of cake in the other, and all of a sudden this dog from across the street came running straight at me.

"I was so startled, I thought he was going to bite me. He wasn't, actually—he was just going for the cake! Anyway, he was big and clumsy and I was little. He knocked me down, scarfed down my cake, as I screamed and hollered. His owner was a neighbor and was really apologetic. But after that—for a long time, anyway— I was afraid of big dogs. I got over it eventually, but I remember just panicking anytime a dog came near me. I was sure it was going to knock me down again, I guess." [13]

Innate Fears

Bad experiences can account for many fears, but not all of them. It is known that many species of animals, including humans, are born with certain instinctive fears. Baby chicks, for example, are born fearing hawks, as a 1951 experiment demonstrated.

Curious whether the shape of a hawk overhead would spark instinctive fear in young birds, psychologist Konrad Lorenz passed a V-shaped object over newly hatched chicks. Instantly, they became agitated and afraid. As one expert explains, "[The chick] has inherited the genetic message—*hawk, danger*—for a certain-shaped shadow, even though he is only a couple of days old and has not talked to his mother and may never see a hawk."[14]

The type of innate fear varies by species. Psychologists say that animals that are frequently preyed on have far more fears than those who are predators, such as lions and wolves. Even so, the higher mammals also have instinctive fears. Some, such as a fear of snakes or a fear of strangers, come at particular ages. Adult chimpanzees, for example, are deathly afraid of snakes— even if they have never seen one before. Younger chimps, however, may simply exhibit curiosity about them.

Human babies become startled and show fear at loud noises almost from birth. Other fears surface later, such as fear of the dark (age three and older), fear of high places (when a baby begins to crawl), and fear of strangers (at six to twelve months). These fears are almost universal—they occur in children all over the world and almost always at the same age. What's more, research has shown that such fears almost always go away as the child grows older.

"Good" Fear

As distressing as acute fear and anxiety can be, psychologists maintain that, in moderation, they are very helpful. For instance, the learned fear of a busy street can make any pedestrian more cautious and, as a result, safer. The anxiety one might feel at the thought of giving a speech to a large group of people may give a person an edge he wouldn't have if he were completely comfortable.

Psychologists have found that a certain amount of fear and anxiety improves performance in a wide variety of situations— from soldiers in battle to a job interview, from a business presentation to pitching in a World Series game. If a person has too little fear, performance is poor; too much fear, and the same result occurs. Thus, moderate amount of fear raises the level of performance.

"I do play better when I'm a little afraid," agrees one high school soccer goalkeeper. "If I'm relaxed, I'm more likely to get scored on. I don't think it's just me, either—it seems like our

Moderate levels of fear and anxiety can improve performance in stressful situations, even on a battlefield.

whole team plays better if we're all a little scared going in to the game."[15]

Phobia: A Destructive Fear

Although moderate anxiety and fear can be extremely constructive emotions, phobias are purely destructive. They not only have no positive effect, but they can become a life-altering nightmare.

As stated earlier, a phobia is a type of fear that is very intense, but at the same time unreasonable considering the circumstances. For instance, Tim's fear of dogs after his experience of being knocked down was not a phobia. For a young boy, his subsequent fear of dogs was a natural, understandable thing. It was not unreasonable in the least for Tim to have been afraid of that dog—or other large dogs he came in contact with.

A phobia is also persistent. It is not a onetime fear; rather, it continues over a long period of time. Most realistic fears go away, unless the person gets the message again and again that the feared

A person with a phobia of dogs will fear all dogs, including friendly ones.

object is dangerous. As he got older, Tim's fear was gradually forgotten as he came into contact with friendly dogs that did not jump on or scare him. Had every dog he met from then on jumped on him, however, his fear of dogs would most likely have continued.

A person with a phobia, however, continues to be afraid. Because the fear is unreasonable, it does not lessen—nor can it be overcome voluntarily. A person with a phobia of dogs would continue to be afraid even if the dogs he met were harmless and nonthreatening. Just the fact that they were dogs would be enough for his fear to persist. Yet even though he knows his fear is unreasonable and illogical, he simply cannot overcome it.

A Disabling Fear

Another key element of phobias is that they are disabling. A person with a phobia will find that her life is significantly affected by the fear. Usually one will avoid any situation that is likely to bring her into contact with the feared object or activity.

"I developed a phobia about eating when I was in fifth grade," says Gilian, now thirty-nine. "It was like one day I woke up and I was scared to death to eat in front of anyone except my family. It was the oddest thing—I still am uncertain why it happened.

"My phobia made it impossible for me to eat lunch at school or eat in a restaurant with my family for more than two years. I was afraid people would look at me, or I'd spill, or I'd have too much food in my mouth and choke. It was horrible—I'd physically feel sick just thinking about eating away from home. If I had to go to a restaurant—if we were on vacation or something—I dealt with it by pretending to have a sore throat or a headache, so I wouldn't have to eat. I was OK if I could just sit there without eating. When I think of all the lunches I missed or birthday parties I didn't go to because I'd have to eat cake and ice cream, I get sad."[16]

Are Phobias the Same as Superstitions?

In some ways, a phobia seems to have some of the same characteristics as a superstition. Like phobias, superstitions are unreasonable. To rap one's knuckles on wood for luck, for example, cannot be explained in logical terms—nor can sidestepping a crack on the sidewalk to avoid being plagued with bad luck.

It is also true that superstitions can sometimes disrupt behavior. A superstitious person who will not take part in a Friday activity if it falls on the thirteenth of the month, for example, is arranging his life around his unreasonable fear of that particular day.

However, psychologists insist that a phobia is much different from a superstition. "There are some very important differences between the two," says one therapist. "For one thing, we don't

Phobias can signficantly affect a person's life. Eating in front of others, being in social situations, or riding in cars are common phobias.

tend to see the intense, almost paralyzing fear of a sidewalk crack or a broken mirror—two subjects of superstitious behavior—as we do in people with phobias. A superstitious person can usually go about his or her business quite easily, where a phobic individual often has severe limitations."[17]

In addition, say experts, unlike phobias, superstitions are not individual. Superstitions are widely held throughout a society or culture. In fact, adults often share their superstitions with younger members of a society. For example, they good-naturedly tell a child not to open an umbrella inside the house because it's bad luck. On the other hand, a person with a phobia, knowing that what she feels is unreasonable and disabling, would certainly not wish to convince others to feel the same unpleasant fear.

A Product of Modern Society?

Another common speculation about phobias concerns their prevalence in society. Psychologists agree that it is difficult to come up with an accurate number of people with phobias. Many won't admit to having a phobia because they are embarrassed or ashamed. Others try to deal with the fear on their own, usually with poor results. Whatever the reason, many experts feel that even the figure of 26 million Americans who have phobias could be a low estimate.

Regardless, the fact that phobias are the most common mental disorders today causes some to wonder about modern society. Are the stresses and pressures of today's hectic lifestyles the cause of so much misery? Although it would be easy to dismiss phobias as a by-product of modern society, researchers say the facts seem to show otherwise.

Chapter 2

History and Early Research

THE TERM *PHOBIA* was not used in the English language until the late 1700s, but the existence of intense, unreasonable fears has been observed for thousands of years. The ancient Greek physician Hippocrates, who lived between 460 and 377 B.C., was one of the first to document such fears.

Flutes and Ditches

One phobia that Hippocrates described involved Nicaros, a man he knew who was terrified of flute music, a common musical entertainment at banquets in ancient Greece:

> When Nicaros used to begin drinking, the girl flute player would frighten him. As soon as he heard the first note of the flute at a banquet, he would be beset by terror, and say that he could scarcely contain himself. During the day, he would hear this instrument without feeling any emotion.[18]

Hippocrates was puzzled, not only because the fear seemed completely unreasonable but because the flute music was only a problem at night. He also commented on

The ancient Greek physician, Hippocrates, was the first to document phobias.

23

another strange fear, that of Nicaros's friend Damocles. "[Damocles] would not go near a precipice," wrote Hippocrates, "or over a bridge or beside even the shallowest ditch, and yet he could walk in the ditch itself."[19]

The Frightening God

It was a Roman medical authority named Celsus who coined the word for the first phobia: *hydrophobia,* which is the fear of water. Celsus, who lived in the first century A.D., was not describing this in terms of a mental disorder, as modern psychologists do. Rather, he was referring to a symptom of the disease rabies. A person in the early stages of that dreaded disease usually experiences throat spasms, pain, and fear at the thought of drinking— or even looking at—water.

Celsus added the word *phobia* as a suffix to the word *hydro,* meaning water. The word *phobia* Celsus took from one of the most frightening of the Greek gods, Phobos. Phobos was a hideous-looking deity with fiery eyes and a wild, snarling mouth. It was said that if soldiers prayed to him on the eve of battle, even their most courageous enemies would be paralyzed with fear. Many Greek soldiers painted Phobos's likeness on their battle shields.

The Roman medical authority Celsus gave the fear of water the name hydrophobia.

Celsus gave what he thought was sound advice to physicians whose patients were suffering from what seemed like a very strange fear:

> There is just one remedy, to throw the patient unawares into a water tank which he has not seen beforehand. If he cannot swim, let him sink under and drink, then lift him out; if he can swim, push him under at intervals so that he drinks his fill of water even against his will; for so his thirst and dread of water are removed at the same time.[20]

"Some . . . Are Mad If They Behold a Cat"

Although Celsus's use of the *-phobia* suffix was not used to identify other intense, unreasonable fears until much later, doctors and writers through the centuries continued to note such fears among people they observed.

William Shakespeare referred to what is known today as a very common phobia in *The Merchant of Venice:* "Some, that are mad if they behold a cat." And in addition to his thorough examination of the physical reaction of fear, seventeenth-century writer Robert Burton documented a wide variety of baffling fears in his friends—from being terrified at the idea of robbers to somehow losing control in church: "He is afraid he shall speak aloud unawares, something indecent and unfit to be said." Burton goes on to describe a man whose intense fears focused on enclosed spaces and crowds:

> If he be locked in a close room, he is afraid of being stifled for want of air, and still carries bisket, acquavitae, or some strong waters about him, for fear of being sick; or if he be in a throng, middle of a church or multitude, where he may not well get out, he is so misaffected.[21]

In his play The Merchant of Venice, *William Shakespeare refers to a common phobia: an unreasonable fear of cats.*

Opening the Floodgates

These early descriptions of unreasonable, intense fears seemed to spur others to describe other irrational fears they'd noted among their friends or relatives—or even in themselves. For instance, in 1794 Samuel Johnson pointed to his own fear of crowds as a reason to be excused from jury

An intense fear of crowds prompted Samuel Johnson to request that he be excused from jury duty.

duty. As he explained, he "came very near fainting . . . in all crowded places."[22]

Others who studied human behavior looked carefully at such descriptions, hoping to find more about this strange (but evidently not rare) phenomenon. Some of them were curious about the nature of such fears and questioned whether they were all symptoms of other problems, as had been assumed for centuries.

One German doctor named Karl Westphal disagreed with that assumption. In 1871 he published an article describing his work with three patients, all of whom were terrified of public places. Westphal coined the term *agoraphobia* from *agora*, the Greek word for marketplace. Westphal also insisted that such an unreasonable fear could be a disorder in itself, not merely a symptom of another problem. This observation greatly interested other researchers.

From Triskaidekaphobia to Ombrophobia

After Westphal's description and subsequent naming of agoraphobia, other doctors pitched in with other fears they had diagnosed in their own patients. As the years went by, the list of phobias grew longer. And each was named by adding a Greek (or sometimes Latin) word to the suffix *-phobia*, since Greek and Latin were considered the scholarly languages. If a person had a fear of rain, for example, the term for her disorder was *ombrophobia* (from *ombro*, the Greek word for rain). A fear of bees was apiphobia, a fear of animals was zoophobia, and so on.

After several decades, the list of phobias identified by doctors and psychiatrists had grown to more than three hundred, including triskaidekaphobia (fear of the number thirteen) and pharmacophobia (fear of medicines). There seemed to be no limit to the number of clinical-sounding terms for phobias.

But instead of being encouraged by the growing list of phobias, some professionals were concerned. By assigning a clinical, difficult-to-pronounce name to each phobia, they complained, weren't they engaging in a never-ending exercise?

"What, really, was the point?" asks one researcher. "Health professionals were really doing the patient a disservice, telling him that his problem can be neatly wrapped up into a nice little Greek word. A little arrogance on the part of scientists—and it's not the first time! See, it's not the same as diagnosing food poisoning or diabetes—where doctors do tests and finally identify what it is that's making the patient so sick—and then treating it accordingly.

"Maybe for some people, simply having a name for their dread helped for a little while, I don't know," he says. "But it certainly didn't help doctors to know how to deal with a phobia just by giving it a fancy name."[23]

Instant Obsolescence

Another complaint about the phobia lists that were so prevalent in the early 1900s was that they were always incomplete. After all, there are virtually thousands of abnormal fears that doctors encounter among their patients, and no list could cover them all. One researcher notes that even the most lengthy list was nowhere close to being all-inclusive:

> It doesn't cover the fear of being alone inside a church (described by a San Diego postman), the fear of dead flowers (described by a Boston receptionist), the fear of clowns (described by a Cleveland broadcaster), or the fear of riding in a car driven by someone else (a widely reported fear most often experienced by professionals such as taxi- or truckdrivers).[24]

Besides the existence of so many specific fears, there are also many phobias that were nonexistent generations ago. Because they are fears of modern phenomena, they have no clinical Greek names. A phobia about fast subway trains or about radiation poisoning, for example, would not be included in such lists.

Two Faces of Phobia

Westphal's demonstration of phobias as disorders, rather than as symptoms of other conditions, was an important breakthrough. However, as scientists in the late nineteenth and early twentieth centuries were realizing, they could not be too quick to dismiss the idea that phobias could be symptoms too. Because the study of human behavior is not an exact science, it is rare for psychologists to come up with ironclad laws governing it.

Although it was certainly true that phobias could be disorders in their own right (as Westphal maintained), it was becoming apparent that they also were present in other mental disorders as symptoms. People suffering from severe depression, for instance, often exhibited phobias. However, it was a newly identified problem first described in 1878 that was the source of an important disagreement among phobia researchers: obsessive-compulsive disorder (OCD).

Frantic Fears

The obsessions experienced by a person with OCD are persistent, troublesome thoughts or fears that can't be ignored. An obsessive person might worry that he has not locked his front door. Even after checking the door and finding it securely locked, he begins to doubt again whether he has locked it. No amount of reasoning can convince him to put the obsessive thought out of his mind.

The compulsive aspect of the disorder has to do with the actions an obsessive person takes. Checking the front door once is normal. Checking it again and again—perhaps fifty or sixty times during the night—is not.

Many people with OCD have a phobia of germs. No matter how many times they wash their hands, they worry that they are somehow being contaminated. One Australian woman was so affected by her phobia, according to one newspaper, that she had little time for anything else but washing each day:

She uses up more than 225 bars of soap on herself every month . . . 400 pairs of surgical gloves, 4,000 plastic bags—which she wears in multiple numbers over the gloves—and 360 rolls of paper towels. She goes through dozens of boxes of laundry detergent every month because she washes her clothes six or seven times before wearing them. "And I can't bear to walk on the floors outside my bedroom. I spread newspapers ahead of me as I walk through the house."[25]

A Big Step

There were some psychiatrists who read cases of obsessive-compulsive behavior and classified them merely as phobias. As late as 1913, in fact, several respected psychiatrists believed that there was no need to separate the two and wrote journal articles that did not distinguish between them.

One famous psychiatrist of the day, however, did not agree. Sigmund Freud did not think OCD was a phobia but, rather, one aspect of a separate disorder. He urged his colleagues to consider that phobias can sometimes appear as a disorder and other times as a part of a larger problem, such as OCD. He noted a few important differences between the two—differences that he said were too important for professionals to ignore when diagnosing and treating such patients.

Sigmund Freud disagreed with psychiatrists who classified obsessive-compulsive disorder as merely a phobia.

Freud insisted that people with obsessions, while suffering from acute phobias, usually engaged in behavior that was repetitive and useless as a way to counteract the fear. Hours spent washing hands, checking and rechecking whether lights are off, and other rituals were an important aspect of the disorder. People with phobias only, however, did not engage in such rituals. They dealt with their fears by avoiding those feared objects or situations.

Freud's findings have held up for more than a century: Most psychiatrists and other researchers agree that phobias can be symptoms or disorders. Making the distinction is critical to psychiatrists and other doctors who are treating a phobic patient.

How Do Phobias Begin?

Besides being curious about the nature of phobias, researchers have been fascinated by various ideas about the origin of the fears. There was a great deal of speculation in the late nineteenth and early twentieth centuries, and various theories were published in medical and psychiatric journals.

At first, some thought that the simplest explanation was that a phobic individual must have had some frightening encounter with the object of fear. A woman who has been thrown from a horse might develop a phobia about horses—it seems logical at first glance.

However, there were immediate problems with this theory: While it may explain some phobias, it does not explain them all. For instance, what about the tens of thousands of people who are thrown from horses and do not develop phobias? Can a traumatic or painful event cause a phobia in one person but leave another unaffected? And what about people who have never even encountered a horse yet still exhibit a phobia of the animals?

Freud's Explanation

Sigmund Freud had strong ideas about the origin of phobias, too—ideas that were very different from what he felt were the simplistic ideas of his day. Freud believed that the roots of a phobia could not be explained by a single event. Instead, the cause was an indirect, often convoluted series of things that was deeply embedded in the phobic person's brain. A phobia, he argued, came about because of unresolved anger or jealousy, together with the guilt that might accompany such feelings. As one psychiatrist explains, "[Freud] believed a phobia was a symbolic expression of repressed feelings and the punishment linked to them in the subconscious."[26]

The most famous case that Freud felt illustrated this phenomenon was that of a five-year-old boy, known as "Little Hans," who had a horse phobia. Hans had not had any frightening encounters with horses, and he lived in a city at a time when horses were part of the everyday landscape. His parents were puzzled; nothing they did could allay his fears.

After observing the boy and analyzing his behavior, Freud concluded that the root of the child's phobia was actually Hans's father. Freud believed that horses, because of their power, their size, and other factors, had become a symbol for his father.

The reason for Hans's aggressive feelings is at the foundation of Freud's psychiatry. He proposed that all little boys go through a stage where they vie with their father for their mother's affection. This stage, termed the Oedipus complex (after a character in an ancient Greek drama), was normal and, Freud believed, something that little boys experience sometimes without realizing it.

Because the feelings of competition and aggression toward one's father make a young boy feel somewhat guilty, he focuses his anxiety on an object that he can more easily avoid. In Hans's case, he focused on horses; he could feel anger and fear toward horses without feeling guilty. Once Hans's childhood development proceeded beyond the Oedipal stage, Freud predicted, the phobia—as well as the reasons for it—would disappear.

Freud's explanation of phobias and the complicated ways they originate was debated and discussed throughout the psychiatric world. Even though there is no way to prove these ideas, many psychiatrists believed in Freud's hypotheses. Although today most researchers do not believe that hidden anxieties and repressed feelings are the basis of all phobias, they do acknowledge that, in some cases, that explanation makes a great deal of sense.

Learning Phobias?

In the early 1920s, phobia research made another stride with the experiments of a psychologist named John B. Watson. Watson's ideas were far different from those of Freud's. He believed that psychology was science and, as such, could be studied objectively. He was leery of the twists and turns of Freud's theories of guilt and anxiety as the cause of phobias. He also did not subscribe to another idea at the time—that people might inherit phobias.

Watson was more confident that such fears were learned, although he believed that a person could "learn" a fear without even being aware of it. His beliefs were based primarily on experiments he conducted with an eleven-month-old baby named Albert.

Psychologist John B. Watson believed that people's fears are learned rather than inherited or developed from guilt or anxiety.

Albert was an easygoing baby who played cheerfully with an assortment of animals in Watson's laboratory, including a rabbit, a white rat, and a variety of dogs. None of the animals frightened him; in fact, the only time the baby showed any fear was when he was startled by a loud noise. When this happened, Albert would scream and cry.

Watson wanted to see if he could "teach" Albert to have a rat phobia. To accomplish this, he took advantage of Albert's fear of loud noise. Whenever Albert held the rat, Watson banged an iron bar just behind the baby's head. It did not take long for Albert to associate the rat with the scary noise. He began to cry whenever the rat was brought close, knowing the noise would soon follow. Even when Watson stopped banging the iron bar, Albert's fear of the rat was very intense. It seemed that Watson had succeeded in creating a phobia where none had existed before.

Phobia by Association

There was an interesting sidebar to Watson's experiments with Albert. After the white rat phobia had been strongly instilled in the baby, the psychologist noticed that something quite unexpected had happened. Today it is known to psychologists as "generalization."

Albert's phobia seemed to spill over onto other things that had characteristics similar to those of the white rat. Playthings that had not been threatening to the child before the experiment now terrified him—a Santa Claus mask with a fluffy white beard, a toy rabbit, a fuzzy coat on a doll. These things now frightened Albert as much as the rat did, Watson realized.

Watson's theory of phobias—namely, that such fears occur when some object is somehow linked to something very unpleasant—became popular, especially with those who were uneasy with Freud's ideas. Watson's work received criticism from some in the psychiatric community, however, primarily because it was based on the behavior of one child. Other efforts to duplicate his work varied in their results, an indication that, like Freud's ideas, Watson's could only explain how *some* phobias originate.

A Difficult Burden

Psychologists today are doubtful that there is any one reason why phobias develop. Recent efforts to understand phobias have concentrated more on profiling people who have phobias and seeing what similarities there are. The profile research has produced some surprising results.

One discovery is that women tend to develop phobias more often than men do, although the significance of this is not yet understood. It has also been found that phobias tend to run in families. And although psychiatrists do not believe that babies are born with phobias, certain people may be more likely to develop them depending on their family history. Some experts think that because people who are generally anxious are more likely to become phobic, it is the tendency toward anxiety that could be genetic. "Think of having a genetic set point [toward anxiety] that is higher than in most other people," says psychiatrist Gail Martz-Nelson. "You have a higher level of general anxiety, and a greater tendency to react to your environment." [27]

But no matter what the cause of the phobia—whether it came from deep in the subconscious or from an environmental or bio-logical factor or from a combination of all these things—it is a very difficult burden to bear. Whatever type of phobia the fear is categorized as—simple, social, or the most crippling of them all, agoraphobia—the phobic person must adjust life around it.

Chapter 3

Social and Specific Phobias

T HE PHOBIAS THAT affect the most people are known as social phobias. Estimates of the number of people in the United States who suffer from them range from 7 to 10 percent of the population. As with any phobia, a social phobia involves an intense, persistent fear. However, instead of being afraid of a particular thing and the imagined harm it could do, the social phobic is afraid of the reaction of other people.

The most common phobias, social phobias, affect 7 to 10 percent of the adults and children in the United States.

A Variety of Frightening Situations

People with social phobias have identified several situations that trigger their fear. For some, it is a fear of blushing or of eating in front of other people. For others, like one Colorado woman, it was a fear that her hands would tremble—thus making her look foolish in front of others.

"I don't write checks in stores," she says. "I don't read the newspaper where other people can see me. I never button my coat when I leave a place, in case my hands would shake so much I couldn't get the button in the hole. I could never eat or drink when I'm out somewhere. I think about how embarrassed I'd be if I dropped something or the food spilled off my fork."[28]

Some people are afraid of being observed, fearing situations such as walking past a group of people or being on the beach in a bathing suit. For one woman with this phobia, her wedding was almost ruined because she was so frightened at the prospect of walking down the aisle.

"It was just as I feared," she recalls. "Everyone in the church was a friend or relative, but even so, I felt as though two hundred pairs of eyes were burning into me. I barely made it to the altar."[29]

Much More than Shy

To some, the term *social phobia* might seem like a clinical-sounding version of "shy." However, experts say that the two are not the same—although they admit that the existence of social phobias was not understood until fairly recently. Only in 1980 was it included in the *Diagnostic and Statistical Manual of Mental Disorders* (DSM-III), the bible of the psychology community.

"The description of social phobia is new," says New York psychiatrist Michael Liebowitz, "but the problem is not. It's been around in several forms, most of them chalked up to shy temperament."[30]

But shyness, say experts, is far different from the terror felt by people with social phobias. "Shy can be a completely normal response in many situations," explains another therapist. "Meeting a blind date or giving an oral report in front of an entire class, maybe mingling with a bunch of new faces at a party—those all can be intimidating situations, and a few butterflies and dryness in the mouth are perfectly normal. But it goes beyond shyness when the terror is so great that you avoid dating or raising your hand in class. You don't go to parties. These types of behavior indicate a social phobia."[31]

Dr. Liebowitz agrees, emphasizing that shyness almost always dissolves once the person gets involved in the activity. "With public speaking, the fear goes away once you start talking, and should get easier each time after that. Just as with dating—after a few dates, you should be more comfortable. Social phobics don't relax or get comfortable—they avoid."[32]

The Results of Social Phobias

A person with a social phobia such as acute shyness is often misunderstood by friends, family, and coworkers. Because he is so uncomfortable with other people, he tries to avoid any situation where he might be included in a group. Such avoidance might

A person with a social phobia might experience terror at the thought of being with a group of people.

look like arrogance or an "I'm too good for you" attitude, say psychiatrists, even though it is nothing of the sort.

"[Social phobics] are not avoiding these [socially interactive] situations because they prefer to be alone," says one researcher. "On the contrary—they want to connect with other people, but intense interpersonal discomfort and self-consciousness make this almost impossible." [33]

Such fear in social situations leads to avoidance, which in turn can lead to a host of other problems. One woman who was in the process of selling her house with the intent to move closer to her grandchildren was so fearful about writing her name in front of people that she canceled her plans. Taking her house off the market and scrubbing her plans of moving was easier for her than summoning the courage to sign her name on a purchase agreement in front of a realtor or banker.

Missed Opportunities

Phobia expert Jerilyn Ross cites another example of avoidance, this one by a fearful nineteen-year-old boy named Jerry. Jerry had been shy all his life, but fear of his social interaction increased dramatically when he entered high school. However, since he was a disciplined student, his parents were not upset by the fact that he preferred to stay home on weekends rather than do things with friends.

By the time he entered college, says Ross, his social phobia had worsened so much that he could barely function:

> During his brief months in college, Jerry didn't make a single friend. At first he could handle attending classes, but soon even that became too difficult and his attendance began to slip. By mid-December he stopped going altogether. He kept up with the reading assignments, but because he missed the class work, his grades plummeted.

> Finally, Jerry got into a pattern of rarely leaving his room except for meals. Usually he would slip into the cafeteria just before it closed and eat alone at a table. . . . After he told his parents he didn't want to stay in college, they made arrange-

ments for him to take a leave of absence. Now that he is home, he stays in his room and listens to music all day.[34]

It is easy to see how a severe social phobia like this can deprive a person of opportunities for education, for dating and meeting people, even for finding a job. Too often, say experts, people with social phobias settle on a job, for example, only because it was the first one they applied for.

"I have seen people who are so grossly underemployed, considering their intelligence, background, and training," says one therapist. "But with a phobia of talking to strangers or something like that, they are trapped.

"They are so panicky and frightened at the thought of going through the steps necessary to land a different job, they aren't able to set up an interview or even to make a phone call to inquire about the possibility. I've had people with the expertise to get maybe a $150,000 job who are working now for minimum wage. They're trapped."[35]

The Most Common Social Phobia

Fortunately, not all social phobias have such profound negative consequences. Although all social phobias by definition are intense and cause a person to avoid the feared activity, some involve situations that are more specific and therefore easier to avoid. For example, a fear of being looked at by other people is very general, since almost any time one is around people, the fear could occur.

The social phobia of speaking in front of a group, however, is far less troublesome; the fear symptoms only occur in that particular circumstance, which usually can be avoided more easily. The fear of public speaking—sometimes termed "performance anxiety" or "stage fright" because it plagues many actors and musicians—is the most common of the social phobias. Psychologists estimate that as many as 40 percent of Americans suffer from it.

"You know the feeling," says one expert. "Your heart is running a marathon but the rest of you is standing still. Your hands are shaking. Your mouth is dry, while the palms of your hands

Stage fright is a common phobia even among performers.

are dripping wet! The butterflies in your stomach feel like a 747. . . . There is an ominous feeling that something bad is going to happen."[36]

Audience or Predators?

People with performance anxiety have a great deal of difficulty being the center of attention. Even people who have no problems with shyness or nervousness in other settings have a difficult time when they are the focal point in a group.

Researchers say that this is a very normal, understandable response. It is the same fear that hits all animals when they are in full view of potential predators, when they are vulnerable and alone. In this modern scenario, however, a phobic fears the predators (the audience) not for the sharpness of their teeth but because they have the ability to make him feel foolish.

Those who have suffered from performance anxiety stress that the feelings are not at all the "butterflies" that most people get at the thought of getting on a stage or preparing to speak in front of a group. The mild surge of adrenaline that produces a jittery, excited feeling is actually beneficial, for it gives a little boost of motivation that all performers recognize as helpful. Without that adrenaline surge, there is usually a flatness, a too-relaxed attitude that can often result in a poor performance. As comedienne Carol Burnett quipped, "You show me somebody who's too calm, and I'll show you somebody who's *too* calm!"[37]

But performance anxiety is not the feeling of shy nervousness that is so commonly felt in such situations. In many cases of performance anxiety, the fear is so severe that the phobic person is often unable to go through with a performance or speech—often because of a rapid heartbeat, unsteady legs, or a mouth so dry that speaking is impossible. Many of these phobic people find that they experience these symptoms even when they are only anticipating the performance.

Willard Scott, the longtime weatherman on the *Today* show who has suffered with severe performance anxiety for more than a decade, made this distinction between the two: "I compare it to cutting your fingers as opposed to having a train run over you. The difference is that dramatic."[38]

Singer Carly Simon was so physically sick and anxious before her concerts that she stopped performing for eight years.

In Good Company

Scott is not the only celebrity who battles performance anxiety. Although it may seem surprising that performers, musicians, and actors who actively seek chances to entertain would be victims of such a phobia, psychiatrists say that they are some of the most severely affected by performance anxiety.

Singer Carly Simon, one of many celebrities who are phobic in public situations, found herself so physically sick and anxious before concerts that she stopped doing live performances for eight years. Sir Laurence Olivier, one of the most famous actors of all time, found his social phobia so strong that he was eventually unable to go onstage unless he was medicated.

Some experts theorize that celebrities are often harder hit by social phobias than noncelebrities, simply because, in their minds, they have more to lose by performing poorly. A professional actor who flubs his lines or a concert pianist who hits a wrong chord might be judged more harshly than a person less well known.

"When a person's performance represents his identity," says Dr. Alice Brandfonbrener, a Chicago psychiatrist, "the stakes become so high that it becomes overwhelming every time they perform."[39]

"Bashful Bladder Syndrome"

Social phobias can develop around any activity or situation in which a person feels ill at ease in the presence of others. One social phobia that is becoming increasingly common is the fear of using a public bathroom. According to recent statistics from the University of Michigan Medical Center, "bashful bladder syndrome," as it is called, affects 10 percent of American men. (Although women can sometimes be affected by this, men are far more likely to experience the phobia since men's rooms are set up in a more open arrangement.)

The effect of this phobia, say doctors, is an inability to urinate even though one feels the need. Although it results in physical discomfort, bashful bladder syndrome is not a physiological disease. "There's nothing wrong with these people medically," says one expert. "But their anxiety about being around others, or being walked-in on, interferes with their ability to urinate."[40]

The severity of the phobia varies a great deal. One person might be able to use a stall instead of a urinal and is therefore not inconvenienced too much. However, some sufferers cannot even use a stall unless they are certain that the bathroom is empty. They might spend long amounts of time waiting until everyone else has left the bathroom before they can use it.

In its extreme form, this phobia makes it impossible for a person to use any bathroom other than his own, no matter how private it is. Because the fear is so strong, a phobic will endure tremendous discomfort for hours rather than use another bathroom. Eventually, many with this phobia become practically homebound.

"We've had patients who wouldn't go anywhere that would require them to be away from home for any significant time," says phobia counselor Joseph Himle. "We've even had patients who bought their homes near where they worked so that they could go home whenever they had to urinate."[41]

Heartbreaking Consequences of Social Phobias

It is not surprising that many people who are troubled with a social phobia find their lives enormously difficult. Being terrified of groups results in a phobic's avoiding parties and get-togethers, as well as important family events such as weddings or graduations.

A social phobic who avoids all gatherings of friends and family will lead a lonely life.

"I wanted so much to be there for my son Charlie's graduation," says Clare. "I knew I couldn't handle it because of my social phobia. I was terrified at the thought of seeing someone I knew and having to talk.

"Before that day, I guess I thought I could sort of rearrange my life to accommodate my fears, and it wasn't too bad. But that day as I watched my husband wave goodbye to me as he left the house with his camera slung over his shoulder, I cried for hours. I thought to myself, this is no way to live. It was like my husband and my son didn't even stop to consider whether I'd go—I'd missed so many family outings that it was just assumed I couldn't. They were right, but it was heartbreaking. I felt like our family was really two people, that in many ways I was as good as dead to them." [42]

The feeling of having their lives so distorted by fear that they can't function is a common one among social phobics. Because they can't talk themselves out of the fear or overcome it logically, they feel cut off and alone. Often, this loneliness and frustration causes them to use—and abuse—drugs and alcohol as a means of

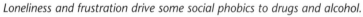

Loneliness and frustration drive some social phobics to drugs and alcohol.

relieving those feelings. Between 30 and 50 percent of problem drinkers started using alcohol because of a social phobia or other anxiety.

"Without help, the person who suffers with a severe social phobia is leading only a partial life," says one woman who suffered for twenty years with a fear of eating in front of others. "You are a paper cutout in a three-dimensional world. I look back on that part of my life like it belonged to someone else, to a complete stranger. No one can understand how crippling it is, I think, unless you've been there yourself."[43]

Chapter 4

Simple Phobias

THOUGH THEY SHARE some characteristics with social phobias, simple phobias are far more specific. A person with a simple phobia is afraid of a particular situation or thing, such as spiders, being in a closed space, hypodermic needles, or heights. And because it is specific, it is often easier to avoid than a social phobia.

The fear that is felt with simple phobias is no less intense than that of a social phobia, however. A man who is afraid of the number thirteen, for example, would experience the same heart-pounding dread if he were on the thirteenth floor of a building as a social phobic might feel if he were asked to give a sales presentation.

Both Commonplace and Unique

Psychiatrists have found that people can have simple phobias about anything. Many phobias are commonplace, such as fear of an animal or fear of going to the doctor. However, some researchers have uncovered some phobias that are far less common, such as the Boston man who was terrified of bathwater or the Iowa teenager who had a severe phobia about seeing anyone's bare toes—including her own.

Jerilyn Ross, a Washington, D.C., phobia expert, once worked with a woman who was afraid of anything having to do with pipes and plumbing. If a water heater in her house broke, she was terrified—and she quickly sold the house rather than have a plumber come in to repair the problem. Another patient had a phobia about anything relating to the state of Wisconsin. "She wouldn't go into a supermarket," explains Ross, "unless her husband went in first and checked out where all the cheeses came from." [44]

Where Do They Come From?

Odd as some of these situations sound, they produce in phobic people the same numbing fear that a phobia of dogs or heights, for example, does to another person. It is important to remember, however, that all phobias are by nature a fear that is far out of proportion to reality. Even the more commonplace dog phobia is unreasonable, because intense physical fear is felt when there is no danger such as when a person sees a picture of a dog.

Simple phobias seem to occur more often in women than in men, and they can begin at any age. Many of them can be traced

A picture of a dog can produce fear in a person with a phobia of dogs.

to a particular incident, such as a dog phobic having been bitten as a child or a person who is afraid of heights having fallen from a ledge or tree.

As convenient an explanation as that would be for psychiatrists, however, it is also true that many simple phobias cannot be traced to a specific origin. No one can explain, for example, why a man who has never been out of the city could break out in a cold sweat at the thought of an alligator, or why a woman who has never been hurt or attacked by birds develops a phobia of them.

But some psychiatrists maintain that if enough was known about a person's background—especially his or her early childhood—it would be possible to uncover reasons for almost every specific phobia. A phobia about enclosed spaces, for example, need not have developed because of a traumatic event such as being trapped all day in a dark cave or locked for hours in a closet.

"It might be something as seemingly inconsequential as having a difficult time getting out of a strange bathroom," says one woman who has severe claustrophobia. "I think that was my problem. My family was visiting friends, and I was only four or five. I went off to the bathroom and couldn't figure out how to open the door again.

"It was only a minute or two, and I figured it out. But it must have scared me enough that that same panic I felt then has returned whenever I'm in a tight space. I was in therapy several years ago because of this, and it was only because I underwent hypnosis that I even recalled this event—my parents didn't even remember me telling them it had happened!"[45]

Phobias That Never Happen

Although the idea that all phobias are learned or acquired from experiences in one's past is an interesting one, many researchers are skeptical. After all, they say, such a theory does not account for the large number of people whose frightening experiences and anxious moments have not resulted in phobias.

One Chicago policeman who was attacked by geese as a child says that he has vivid memories of the incident but insists that he has no phobia.

"I was knocked down by these five geese at my Uncle Pete's farm," he says. "I remember being so frightened. I didn't know what was going to happen to me. I kept thinking, 'Do geese eat kids?' I didn't know. They were all wings and beaks, hissing and making these scary noises, flapping their wings and running toward me.

"But no, I've got no phobia about birds—or anything else I'm aware of," he shrugs. "I can't say that I'd jump at the chance to go into a pen with a bunch of geese, but I could do it if I had to." [46]

Animal Phobias

Although researchers are divided over the "why" of simple phobias, they know a great deal more about the "who" and "when," especially when it comes to animal phobias. They are by far the most common of the simple phobias, and they surface at a fairly early age, usually beginning by age twelve. Boys and girls are equally likely to have an animal phobia at that age; however, women are twice as likely as men to develop such a fear later in life.

The sight of a snake or other animal can cause sheer panic in a person with an animal phobia.

Most people with an animal phobia are afraid of one type of animal rather than animals in general. A person might fear spiders, dogs, bees, or cockroaches but not all of them. And, remarks one researcher wryly, among the most common phobia-causing animals, "with the exception of snakes and some individual dogs, none poses much of a threat to a human being equipped with the minimal defense of sneakers."[47]

Even so, the reaction of a phobic person who comes into contact with the feared animal is not the same reaction as a person who may be squeamish or nervous about a particular animal, say psychiatrists. At its most severe, an animal phobia can cause the worst form of panic, sometimes even resulting in a person putting herself in real danger to avoid the irrational, imagined danger. Consider these four separate cases of women with a severe phobia of spiders:

> A spider-phobic woman screamed when she found a spider at home, ran away to find a neighbor to remove it, trembled in fear, and had to keep the neighbor at her side for two hours before she could remain alone at home again; another spider-phobic found herself on top of the refrigerator in the kitchen with no recollection of getting there. A third threw herself off a galloping horse when [a spider] fell on her off a tree branch. Yet another, who could not swim, jumped out of a boat into the sea to escape a spider.[48]

A Variety of Effects

Of course, just as phobias can range in severity, they also differ in the degree to which they affect a person's life. As mentioned earlier, simple phobias are specific to a particular object or event. In many cases, the fact that they are specific makes it much easier to avoid the object or situation that is feared. A man who has the not-uncommon phobia of dead bodies, for instance, can avoid wakes and funerals and thus prevent phobic reactions. A woman who has a cat phobia can pick and choose who she visits based on their choice of pet.

On the other hand, some simple phobias are not as easily managed by avoidance. Phobias involving thunderstorms, for example, or darkness, are almost impossible to avoid unless a person rearranges his whole life so that he doesn't encounter them too often. The storm phobic tries to cope by playing loud music on the stereo if there is a storm nearby. A person who has a fear of the dark copes by pulling the shades when evening comes and keeping the lights on all night.

"Although it *can* be done," says one man whose wife lived with a fear of the dark for thirty years, "it's very, very difficult. It means rearranging your whole life so you aren't out at night. That means turning down invitations to go out for dinner, and it means going to matinees instead of evening movies. It means feeling really silly sometimes and frustrated other times, and being embarrassed about confiding your fears to your friends."[49]

Other Effects of Severe Phobias

Another effect of a severe simple phobia can be an obsessive-compulsive disorder that centers around the feared object. Says one psychiatrist who has studied people with animal phobias,

> Patients search for the feared animal wherever they go. The slightest hint of its presence will disturb them where the average person would not notice it. Some of them are plagued by recurrent nightmares of the animals they fear. They dream that they are surrounded by large spiders or swooping birds from which they cannot escape.[50]

This can often make the transition from fear of the animal itself to the obsessive anxiety of contamination from coming in contact with the animal. Researcher Fraser Kent tells of one spider-phobic woman who was so worried about

A deep-seated fear of spiders can cause a person to see spiders everywhere and to take extreme measures to avoid contact.

what would happen if a spider entered her home, that she began a never-ending ritual of washing, cleaning, and frequently patrolling her windows and doors:

> She was so afraid of spiders "that when I sweep the floor, I can just imagine them running up the handle of the broom." She dusted and vacuumed her small home twice a day to make sure spiders never invaded it or "got settled in." Food coming from the grocery store was systematically brushed clean and the bags were burned "because that's one way spiders can get all over everything, coming in with all that food." She was wary of visiting friends or of shopping where people were not as meticulous as she.[51]

Surprisingly, most animal phobics are not actually frightened that the animal itself will harm them. Asked what it is that they fear the most about encountering the animal—whether it is a bee, a snake, a large dog, or any other animal—the majority feel that their own personal worst-case scenario is far worse than being stung, bitten, or otherwise attacked. According to psychiatrists, phobic people are most afraid that they will panic or will suffer dire effects from the contact such as having a heart attack or going insane.

The Fear of Dentists

Although pain is not the animal phobic's worry, it is definitely the number one fear among those with a phobia of dentists. This fear is common; it is estimated that 25 million Americans are so terrified at the idea of going to the dentist—even for a cleaning—they can't bring themselves to go.

The way people handle this phobia is the same way they handle other phobias: avoidance. However, in the case of dentists, the avoidance is far more damaging than in other phobias. Dentists occasionally see patients whose fear has kept them out of the dentist's chair for decades—and because of that, their teeth are rotting.

People often lose their teeth or need to have extensive work done because they put off going to the dentist so long. One thirty-four-year-old man's dental phobia was so severe that he

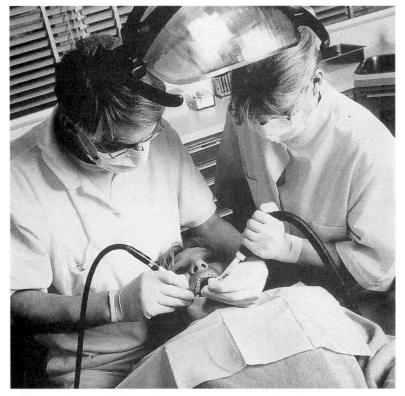

Approximately 25 million Americans have a phobia about dentists.

took painkillers and antibiotics for six months before he could get up the nerve to see a dentist about an abscessed tooth. By that time, several teeth had to be removed.

In Royal Company

The fear of going to a dentist is an old one—quite possibly it has existed since there were dentists. A reference from 1538 describes how Queen Elizabeth of England was in a great deal of pain from a toothache. The queen "had no Intermission day or Night, and it forced her to pass whole Nights without taking any Rest." However, the queen was not willing to see a dentist—known as a "surgeon" in those days—for she feared that more than the pain itself. It was not until the bishop of London presented a very curious plan that the problem was solved:

[The bishop], a Man of high Courage, persuaded her that the pain was not so much, and not at all to be dreaded; and to convince her thereof told her, she should have a sensible Experiment of it in himself, though he were an old Man, and had not many Teeth to spare; and immediately had the Surgeon come and pull out one of his Teeth, perhaps a decayed one, in her Majestie's Presence. Which accordingly was done; and She was hereby encouraged to submit to the Operation herself.[52]

Queen Elizabeth is said to have feared a visit to the dentist more than the pain of a toothache.

It has been found that people who are the most fearful of pain in the dentist's chair seem to be more likely to experience pain. Research indicates that people who are very fearful appear to have increased sensitivity. Because they are more tense and "ready" for pain, they often are more sensitive than they would be if they were relaxed. In this way, say phobia experts, it is a self-fulfilling prophecy: The worry about pain actually causes the pain.

Pain Is Not the Only Fear

Experts say that the cause of this phobia is frequently a learned one. If one had a bad or unsettling experience with a dentist as a child, he is almost always going to have some anxiety about visiting a dentist in later life.

Some phobics attribute their fear to a lack of control, saying that they feel as though they are unaware of what is going on in their mouth when a dentist is at work.

"It's pretty much your space that's being invaded," says one woman. "Maybe because it's your face—I don't know. But it's really invasive, and you have nothing to say about it. I think that's the biggest fear for me, the lack of having any say-so about what's going on in my mouth, where I can't see what's happening."[53]

When Rachel, a fifteen-year-old, discusses her dental phobia, it sounds like a part of it is a social phobia, too. She maintains that her fear is caused by her being judged—a part of every checkup, she says.

"I just brace myself, waiting for the 'tssk' that I know is coming," she says. "Maybe it's because I have a cavity, or even if I don't, she'll say that I'm not flossing. It's like she's seeing all this stuff in my mouth and she's being grossed out about it. Really, I know it sounds weird, but I feel like I've gone to the doctor without taking a bath, you know? I wouldn't do that! But just the way she says it—I hate it. I don't mind the drilling—I'd rather have five cavities drilled than have her giving me that disapproving, judging look."[54]

The physical symptoms of simple and social phobias are very unpleasant. The fact that the fear is irrational is no indicator of the feelings. The weak-kneed fear, the dread, and the pounding heart—these are very real, very uncomfortable physical responses.

"No one I know would choose to have such feelings," says one youth therapist. "It's not the same as someone who likes to be afraid and therefore goes to a scary movie or makes the decision to ride a particularly ferocious roller coaster. Anyone who's ever been really afraid of anything, really terrified—even for just a few minutes—can empathize with a phobic person, I think."[55]

Yet as difficult as life can be with a simple phobia, there is one type of phobia that is even more frightening, and the symptoms more acute. Psychiatrists agree that agoraphobia is the worst phobia of all. Its physical symptoms and its effects on a sufferer's life are so profound that it is in a class by itself.

Chapter 5

Panic Attacks and Agoraphobia

W HEN RESEARCHER KARL Westphal coined the term *agoraphobia* (Greek for "fear of the marketplace") in 1871, he did so because he felt that the most striking symptom of the fear in his three patients was that it seemed to surface when they walked across open spaces. In describing his patients, Westphal wrote of the "impossibility of [their] walking through certain streets or squares, or [the] possibility of [their] doing so only with resultant dread of anxiety."[56]

At about the same time, Austrian physician Moritz Benedikt was discovering a condition that was very similar but whose chief symptom was not anxiety but dizziness, followed by heart palpitations and sweating. He wondered if it was caused by some irregularity in the eye muscles or even the inner ear. But if so, why did the sensation arise in open, public spaces? He had no answer but called the condition *Platzshwindel*, German for "dizziness in public places."

A woodcut of artist Edvard Munch's 1895 painting Anxiety *captures the dread experienced by phobics.*

A Fear "Cluster"

Westphal's term stuck (the German word was a bit too cumbersome), but his view of the phobia

Agoraphobia is the fear of crowded, public places such as a college campus, shopping malls, restaurants, or movie theaters.

was gradually altered. Agoraphobia, as it is now understood, is not merely a fear of open places; it is the fear of crowded public places that is the condition's most common aspect.

But even that is misleading, say experts. Agoraphobia never refers to a single fear, as would a simple or social phobia. Instead, agoraphobia is considered a "cluster fear," because it always encompasses several different situations. A true agoraphobic fears all (or most) of a large number of things.

To an agoraphobic, public transportation is frightening, whether it is an airplane, a bus, a subway, or a train. Enclosed spaces such as tunnels and bridges are impossible for a sufferer to handle. Malls, say researchers, produce a great amount of fear as well for agoraphobic people, as do restaurants and grocery stores.

Waiting in line—whether at a store or at an amusement park ride—also produces great fear. So does sitting in a shop getting one's hair cut or styled; in fact agoraphobia has sometimes been nicknamed "barber's chair syndrome" because of the large number of people who have difficulty in that situation. People with agoraphobia also have a fear of sitting in a theater or concert hall, especially when their seats are not directly on an aisle.

Besides fearing all or many of those situations, agoraphobics have something else in common. Almost every person suffering with agoraphobia can trace the fear's onset to a particularly terrifying experience called a "panic attack." Far more potent than other physical responses to fears and phobias, the panic attack is considered the highest level of anxiety and fear a human being can experience.

A young mother is pictured enjoying a trip to the market with her daughter. An agoraphobic would be highly fearful of such an outing.

"I'm Going to Die"

Anne, a writer and mother of two, was twenty-seven when she suffered her first panic attack. Up till then, she had led a very healthy life. She had never been sick for more than a day or two and prided herself on keeping fit. She ran three miles several times each week and played tennis regularly with her husband. So when she had what she refers to as "the worst twenty minutes of my life" one sunny afternoon in May six years ago, she was completely baffled.

Anne was driving her younger daughter Lucy to a friend's birthday party. The trip was one she'd made dozens of times. The light traffic and her daughter's high spirits were making the drive easy. However, as she swung off the highway onto the road leading to the house, Anne was suddenly seized by panic so intense she was breathless.

"I'd never felt this way before," she declares. "I couldn't breathe; my chest felt as though my heart was going to explode. I was certain I was having a heart attack, and it was all I could do to pull the car over to the side. I kept thinking, 'I'm going to die; I'm never going to see my family again.' I was dizzy, too—and I was trying to remember all the warning signs I'd read about heart attacks. Was dizziness or feeling as though you're going to faint one of the symptoms?"

Questions

Anne says that the episode lasted perhaps ten minutes, although it felt like an hour or two as she struggled to understand what was happening to her.

"I was breathing so fast and so loud that Lucy was yelling to me, 'Mommy, what's the matter!' But I couldn't answer—I just felt as though I was fighting for my life. And as the minutes were going by, I felt as though my heart was slowing down.

"I gradually started breathing normally—at least slowly enough to convince myself I wasn't going to die immediately. I'm not kidding, though. All I could think about was turning the car around and driving back home, where it was safe. My husband was there, my home was there. I just had to get out of that car!

An enclosed place such as a car or crowded surroundings such as bumper-to-bumper traffic can initiate a panic attack in agoraphobics.

"And that," says Anne, "was the start of the most horrible part of my life. I didn't know what was wrong, but I had a terrible feeling that it was very serious, if not fatal. Was it my heart? A stroke or something? I didn't know. I just knew that I had just had the closest call of my whole life, and I was lucky to have gotten the two of us home."[57]

"About as Bad as a Coronary"

A panic attack is terrifying. People who have had them frustrate themselves trying to explain the feeling; they say there are no words to convey the sheer terror. *Newsweek* writer Eloise Salholz, who researched a story about agoraphobics, says of a panic attack, "It is, say those who know, about as bad as a coronary, except that you can get one every week, or oftener, for your whole life."[58]

The attack itself lasts anywhere from five minutes to an hour, although, like Anne, sufferers claim they seem to go on for much longer. The fear and dread is only part of the attack; people who've had them say that they usually become dizzy, nauseated, and feel that they cannot catch their breath. Their muscles often feel stiff, making movement difficult.

One young New York woman who had a panic attack while watching a movie ran into the bathroom thinking she was going to be sick. After undoing her jeans, she soon found that she had another problem.

"To my astonishment," she says, "I couldn't zip them up again. My arms and hands were locked, unable to move. I had to stagger out of the bathroom half-dressed to get help, and I wound up in a hospital emergency room." [59]

Going Insane?

On top of all these sensations, a panic attack also causes sufferers to feel that they are insane, that what they are feeling is very different from reality. This eerie feeling is known as "depersonalization," and doctors agree that it is difficult to explain if one has never experienced it.

Depersonalization makes people feel unreal, strange, and disembodied—as if they were cut off from their surroundings or watching themselves from another perspective. People at the height of a panic attack also say that they feel completely out of control; all they can think about is running away from wherever they are at the time as fast as they can. And because the sensations are so violent and so foreign, they are convinced that they are dying.

One teenager describes feeling the necessity to bolt when he was shopping in a mall one day:

> Suddenly, I couldn't catch my breath. If I didn't get into daylight soon, I was going to pass out, be sick, have a heart attack. I ran for the nearest outdoor exit and pushed through the doors. There I stayed, plastered to a bench, staring at the sky, taking slow deep breaths and wondering if I was going insane. [60]

"She Had Let Me Down"

It is not hard to understand why, with the severity of the physical and psychological symptoms of a panic attack, the usual response is to seek medical help. Many rush to emergency rooms certain that they've had a heart attack or stroke—and are stunned to find that they haven't. Experts now estimate that more than one-third of all people brought into emergency rooms suspected of having a heart attack have actually suffered a panic attack.

Unfortunately, when no physical cause for the episode is discovered in the emergency room, there is confusion. For Anne, whose initial panic attack while driving sent her to her family doctor for a thorough exam, the lack of answers was frustrating.

"I left her office feeling that she had let me down, that somehow she just didn't understand," says Anne. "When I got home, I called the heart clinic my dad went to after his heart attack three years before and scheduled an appointment. I was thinking, 'And if I don't get answers there, I'll find someone else until I get this heart thing figured out.' At that point, money and time were no object. I'd do whatever it took."[61]

"What If It Happens Again?"

One of the most confusing things about a panic attack is that it comes without warning. Unlike the person with a simple or social phobia, there is no threatening object or situation. There is no spider, no dog, no mouse. There is no speech or performance that

Those experiencing a panic attack for the first time often believe they are suffering from a heart attack and seek emergency medical attention.

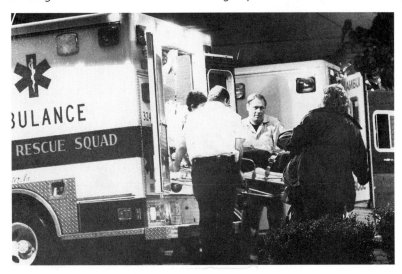

causes the panic. That is one reason why people who have had panic attacks say they feel so disoriented. They feel a strong need to run away—but from what?

That is the key to the beginnings of agoraphobia. A person who has had a random panic attack is so frightened by the experience that, in her mind she associates it with whatever she was doing when it occurred. And because the experience was so uncomfortable, she begins to feel nervous the next time she is in that situation.

"For me, it was driving," says Anne. "I was nervous the next day when I got in the car. I remember putting my seat belt on and thinking, 'God, what if it happens again?' I could feel myself getting afraid just thinking about it. So I went back in the house and asked my husband if he'd go to the store so I didn't have to. And the next day after that, when my son wanted me to take him somewhere, I made up an excuse so I didn't drive then, either."[62]

From Panic to Agoraphobia

Psychiatrists say that most people who suffer one panic attack experience more of them as time goes by. Whereas the first attack may have occurred when the person was driving, a second attack may hit while at work or while shopping. And as that person rearranges his life to avoid those situations—for fear that he may suffer another—he becomes more and more isolated.

This isolation and fear, brought about by the fear of a panic attack, is the gist of agoraphobia. Some experts even call the condition "a fear of fear." More than 75 percent of the time, they say, agoraphobia begins within a year of the first panic attack. By that time, many have already suffered a second or a third.

"My second panic attack was waiting in line at the Gap to pay for a shirt," Anne remembers. "I started getting that tingling feeling and feeling kind of 'out of body' again, and my heart was beating out of my chest. I felt myself going numb around my mouth, and I threw down the shirt and just left. And that was the end of me in stores.

"I wasn't driving, I wasn't going to stores or anywhere there were lines or crowds. It wasn't long before I was staying home all

After experiencing two or three panic attacks in public, many people become virtual prisoners in their own homes, fearful of when the next attack might come.

day, every day. That's where I felt the safest, and that was what I had to do. It was survival. I can positively state that I rarely left my house for almost two years."[63]

Such a case history is not uncommon, say psychiatrists. There are many people who become virtual prisoners of their homes as their worlds shrink smaller and smaller. For some, being home is "safe." For others who may suffer a panic attack while at home, they may confine themselves to a part of the house, or just a room.

This self-imposed confinement can go on for years. One Manhattan woman who suffered a panic attack while at the beauty parlor in 1948 went straight home and did not leave her apartment for forty-six years—and then it was only because she fell and broke her leg. People who had lived in the same apartment building as her for decades say that they had assumed the apartment was vacant because in all that time they had never seen anyone coming or going.

Ranges of Severity

Not all agoraphobics are afflicted so severely. Some find that they can manage to carry on a fairly normal life by making a few critical adjustments. For example, some agoraphobics find that they can travel several miles from home before feeling anxious, so they limit their outings accordingly. Some who have experienced panic while driving find that keeping the windows wide open (even during the winter) helps, as does chewing gum or sucking on hard candy.

Other agoraphobics start carrying a cane or an umbrella, to give themselves a sort of "crutch." And some only feel safe leaving home if a particular "safe" person—usually a spouse or sibling—comes with them.

"I'm the only one who can get my husband Don to leave the house," says one Minneapolis woman. "He can manage work all right, but anywhere else is hard. I have to stay right with him, all the time. He calls me 'Crutch' sometimes, and I know he's a little embarrassed about it. But there are just some things he needs to get out for—going to our grandson's baptism was one. I feel bad for Don, I really do. It's been many years since he's been this way, and I often wonder if he even remembers that at one time he was the kind of man who would jump in the car and take a drive, or go for a walk with the dog, just spontaneously." [64]

Who Gets Agoraphobia?

Researchers estimate that between 6 and 10 percent of Americans suffer from some degree of agoraphobia. They stress that estimates are difficult because many agoraphobics don't seek treatment for their fears.

"Most agoraphobics do make the rounds of doctors because of physical symptoms they experience during panic attacks, but because we are often told that there is nothing wrong, or worse, 'It's all in your head,' we retreat," notes a former agoraphobic. "So there are legions of people out there who are just like I was, sort of invisible to the world, just staying where they feel safe." [65]

Women are more likely than men to suffer panic attacks and agoraphobia; nearly 80 percent of diagnosed agoraphobics are women. The average first panic attack occurs between the ages of sixteen and thirty-two. The average panic-attack sufferer gets them two to four times a week, but people have been known to have as many as several in one day, or as few as one a year.

What Causes Agoraphobia?

It seems that there is a strong likelihood that agoraphobia—or the tendency to develop the condition—runs in families. People who are high strung or nervous also tend to be vulnerable to panic disorders. Most agoraphobics have a parent, sibling, or other relative who also had the problem. Researchers say that if one identical twin is agoraphobic, most of the time the other will be too.

Research shows that almost 80 percent of diagnosed agoraphobics are women and that their first panic attack occurred between the ages of sixteen and thirty-two.

The first panic attack for most agoraphobics seems to occur within six to twelve months of a very stressful situation—good or bad. It might be the death of a parent or friend, a move, a job change, or the birth of a baby. Many psychologists are unwilling to focus completely on either hereditary or environmental factors, believing that the cause is probably a combination of the two.

Misunderstood

People who have suffered a random panic attack and agoraphobia are often misunderstood—not only by health professionals but by their families and friends. Many agoraphobics say that it is embarrassing to explain the panic they feel in certain situations to anyone except family members.

"I just stopped going to things," says one woman flatly. "I told people I was sick, or I was busy. At first, they probably believed me, but after a while most of them just stopped calling. Maybe they think I've found new friends, or they think I'm being aloof or something. I guess I'd rather have them think those things than explain to them what it really is—that I feel like if I go away from home I'll die. Then they'd think I was crazy, and I couldn't stand that." [66]

Even though many agoraphobic people feel safe staying at home with family members, the situation is often stressful for spouses and children, who don't really understand why life has changed so dramatically. Therapists point out that, while the husband of a woman with agoraphobia may be understanding and sympathetic at first, he might become impatient as the months drag on with no sign of improvement.

"My husband was willing to shuttle the kids around to ballet and piano lessons when he could," says Anne. "But he wasn't always around, and so there were weeks when the kids didn't go. I remember Lucy looking at me like 'Hey, you're not sick, why don't *you* drive us?' And I think even [my husband] Ed felt that way after a couple of weeks. I think if I had had a real disease like mono or the flu or something, he'd have been fine, and so would the kids.

"What guilt I felt then! I'd try to tell them that I just couldn't, that it felt so awful to think about driving or going out. But really, it's impossible to communicate that to anyone who's never had a panic attack. He'd be like, 'Just talk yourself out of it, Anne. Just shake it off.' But you just can't. I tried to tell him, but I knew my words sounded whiny and lame. Quite honestly, there were times that I felt Ed might leave for good, and part of me wouldn't have blamed him."[67]

It is not hard to understand why many agoraphobics, especially those whose condition keeps them tied to home, suffer crushing bouts of depression. They are more prone to abuse drugs and alcohol and are more likely to commit suicide than other people. They often feel that they are alone and out of place; doctors repeatedly tell them there's nothing wrong and even family members don't always understand.

Yet as dire as agoraphobia sounds, it is very treatable, say psychiatrists. The hardest part is often realizing that the problem is not heart or stomach trouble—nor "all in their head." A great deal of information about panic attacks and phobias of all kinds has been learned in the last decade. Not only can therapists today diagnose agoraphobia and other phobias accurately, they can also determine the best way of dealing with them.

Chapter 6

Overcoming Phobias

IN HER BOOK *Triumph over Fear*, Jerilyn Ross cites recent studies that indicate that less than one-fourth of people with phobias are getting treatment. This occurs despite the fact that psychiatrists and other therapists agree that phobias—including the most severe cases of agoraphobia—are highly treatable today. Why are more than 75 percent of people with phobias not getting help?

A Wide Range of Possibilities

There are several reasons why people with phobias do not seek help. However, many people who suffer from panic attacks and agoraphobia do not get help not because of a lack of trying. Many *do* try very hard to find out the cause of their problem. The trouble is, most people who have suffered a panic attack are so terrified by the physical sensations that they concentrate on those—chest pains, rapid heartbeat, insomnia, or digestive problems.

When a person in the throes of a full-blown panic attack shows up at an emergency room and finds that his symptoms are not caused by a heart attack, he is often confused. One man said that he was relieved at first, but after his second and third panic attacks, he was angry.

"I was mad that they hadn't found what certainly seemed like a heart attack. I remember being really teed off that the first guy hadn't caught it. But then, the next doctor I went to couldn't find anything either. He says I'm healthy, but I feel terrible. So then what do you do?"[68]

What a lot of people with agoraphobia do is resign themselves to their belief that there is no cure. They stop looking for answers and withdraw; they avoid everything that might cause another panic attack. Others are more fortunate and eventually find help. However, says Jerilyn Ross, the delay caused by health professionals misdiagnosing agoraphobia is a hefty one. "On average," says Ross, "it takes the phobic eight to ten years to find appropriate treatment, and in that time the average person sees ten health professionals."[69]

Hardly Worth the Time

Another reason many phobics don't get treatment is that some phobias are not intense enough to interfere with their lives. A phobia of mountains when one lives on the plains of Kansas, for example, is unimportant in the day-to-day life of that person—and hardly worth taking the time and effort to cure. That's a big reason why some phobics—especially those with animal fears or certain other simple phobias—don't bother getting treatment.

"Getting rid of a phobia isn't just something to do because you have nothing better to do," says phobia expert Manuel Smith. "If you're living in downtown Chicago and have a snake phobia, why bother trying to get rid of it? The chances of seeing a snake in downtown Chicago are highly unlikely."[70]

The phobic person who doesn't get treatment because he simply doesn't need it is in a fortunate situation. However, there are many people with phobias who don't get help because they are too embarrassed. Some researchers feel that men are more apt to hide phobic feelings—which could explain the statistics that indicate that women are more prone to phobias.

Many people who finally seek treatment after years of battling a phobia admit that embarrassment was what delayed their getting help. "I wish I'd done it sooner, now," says one fifty-five-year-old man. "But you know, you just imagine your friends and what they'd say. It was silly, letting that get in the way."[71]

Tackling a Phobia on One's Own

There are a variety of ways that phobias are overcome, say experts, and one of the most common may seem surprising, considering

Experts say many phobias such as fear of flying can be overcome simply by avoiding the feared object or place and choosing alternatives.

how powerful many phobias are. Even so, tackling one's own fear (or the source of the fear) can certainly be done.

In these situations, the phobia is almost always a simple or easily identified social one, and its "cure" can be simply a means of avoidance that does not excessively curtail one's activities. For instance, if a person has a fear of snakes, he could move to a region of the country where snakes are rare. People who have a phobia about airplanes can choose a career in which it is not necessary to travel.

Yet even if one's chosen profession does involve heavy traveling, someone who fears flying can find alternatives. Sports announcer John Madden is a phobic who can't avoid travel; he does play-by-play for the National Football League in cities throughout the United States. Refusing both to fly and to give up his job, Madden solved his problem by outfitting a large, comfortable bus and hiring a driving staff. Crisscrossing the country on wheels

—racking up more than fifty thousand miles during the four months of the football season each year—he is able to avoid the panic he would fear in an airplane yet still arrive refreshed and on time for games throughout the week.

The most famous "self-cure," according to phobia researchers, involved the noted and somewhat mysterious Howard Hughes in the 1950s. Hughes suffered from various phobias, especially in his later life, but according to staff members, one particular fear caused him a great deal of anxiety when he was living in the penthouse of the Desert Inn in Las Vegas, Nevada. The hotel across the street from the Desert Inn was for sale, and the realtors had created a 189-foot-high sign in front of it, announcing its availability.

Hughes was seized by a fear that the large sign was going to blow down onto his penthouse suite. He fretted about it during the day and lay awake at night imagining the disaster. He sent his aides to speak to the building's owners, asking

Reclusive millionaire Howard Hughes suffered from a number of different phobias.

that they remove the sign—or at least make a smaller one. The owners refused, and Hughes's phobia increased—until he thought of a "cure." He wrote out a large check to buy the hotel himself, and removed the sign.

Psychoanalysis

Not every simple or social fear can be successfully avoided, however. A man who is afraid of eating in front of other people, for example, can avoid that situation only by severely limiting his social life. A woman who fears a common animal such as a dog or a bird cannot easily avoid those things, no matter how willing she is to relocate. A man who cannot use bathrooms other than his own will also suffer great inconveniences, which could limit employment and travel. And as long as an agoraphobic has the fear of a random episode of panic—something she can't control—she will be fearful.

For many years, it was believed that all fears originated in a patient's past—in his childhood, his family life, even in his subconscious mind. Experts believed that the only way to be cured of a phobia was for one to submit to intense psychotherapy, during which a psychiatrist could explore the patient's innermost thoughts and experiences until he uncovered the source of the phobia. Once the underlying cause was brought into the daylight, it was thought, the phobia could be mastered.

Although a valuable tool for many psychological disorders, psychoanalysis for phobic patients had several drawbacks. Often, the sessions went on for months—and even years—without the psychiatrist finding the root of the phobia. This was both costly and frustrating for the patient. In fact, even when an event was uncovered that might account for the phobia, the patient frequently did not master his fear.

One study found that patients who had undergone intensive therapy for even ten or fifteen years showed only slight improvement with their fears; another found that only 13 percent of phobics were free of symptoms after intensive therapy. As psychiatrist Donald Goodwin comments, "The recovery rate for untreated patients is usually higher than this."[72]

Behavior Therapy

In the early 1960s, some psychologists began using a different approach with their phobic patients. Although they agreed that there were some phobias that were a symptom of other, deep-seated psychological problems, most phobias were not. They felt it was possible to treat the phobia while forgoing analysis for most of their phobic patients. By helping a patient learn to face the objects of his phobia and to tolerate the symptoms those objects can trigger, psychologists found that the fear and anxiety would almost always dissolve.

Today, behavior therapy—in its various forms—is recognized as the most effective treatment for all three types of phobias.

Either alone or combined with certain medications, behavior therapy has been extremely successful. The trick, say therapists, is to find the type of behavior therapy that works best in each case, since there are individual differences between patients.

Desensitization

One common behavior therapy technique is called "desensitization." The key to desensitization is providing a phobic person with gradual exposure to the thing or situation he most fears until it loses its power to frighten him.

A therapist usually begins by having the patient construct a phobia hierarchy—a type of list that grades various aspects of the phobia from "least fearful" to "most fearful." A man with a snake

Treatment of a phobia sometimes starts with the patient looking at a photo of the feared object or environment.

phobia, for instance, might list "seeing a picture of a snake" as the least-feared aspect of his phobia, while "standing five feet from a snake" would be more feared. Actually holding a snake (which any snake phobic would find utterly impossible to imagine himself doing) would certainly be the most feared item on the hierarchy.

The next step would be for the therapist to help the patient visualize the least fearful item on his list. The patient is taught some muscle-relaxation techniques that will put him at ease as he gradually moves up the list. This step-by-step advancement through the hierarchy, combined with the relaxation techniques, will eventually allow the patient to imagine even the top item on his list without fear.

Beyond Imagination

Having learned to imagine phobic situations without fear, the patient's next step goes beyond imagining. In the same gradual stages that he accomplished his visualization, he begins real-life exposure to the feared situation or object. As in visualization therapy, he is encouraged to stay calm and focused using deep relaxation techniques.

At first, the patient might merely look at pictures of snakes or draw them. Later he might stand in a room and watch someone hold a snake. He might be asked to imagine touching the snake. A therapist would ask him at each stage to explain the thoughts he was having; is he afraid or merely anxious? Little by little, he would increase his exposure until he can approach the snake a few feet at a time. Eventually, he can hold the snake without fear.

Many with animal phobias have been cured in a session or two, and often they even surprise themselves by their new way of looking at creatures they once had nightmares about. Jane Simmons, a woman who recently attended a three-hour therapy session about spiders, was astounded at the difference she felt after the therapy. Whereas before she couldn't even think about going on a picnic for fear that she'd see a spider, she now finds them lovable. Says Simmons, cradling a large fuzzy spider at the London Zoo, "I'd rather die than kill one."[73]

Desensitization and Social Phobias

Behavior therapy techniques are usually very successful with social phobias, too. At the University of Michigan Medical Center, therapists have designed a desensitization program for men whose social phobia about using public bathrooms has created problems in their lives. The treatment, which involves about ten sessions, requires all participants to arrive at their weekly session with a full bladder.

The men start out by getting accustomed to tiny bathrooms in remote corners of the campus, and gradually they work themselves up to large, more crowded ones. In early sessions, the therapist stands outside the restroom door and reassures the patient that no one will come in while he's using the restroom. Once the patient feels secure enough to start urinating, the therapist moves just inside the door, then closer and closer until he's standing just behind the patient—quite similar to the environment in a large public restroom.

"I might even fidget around or make nasty comments about how long it's taking," explains one therapist, "or even bump against the patient to simulate a real-life situation."[74] The desensitization has proved effective with the vast majority of patients, virtually eliminating their phobias.

Flooding

Another technique that has gained popularity with therapists in recent years is known as "flooding." Whereas desensitization is a gradual, step-by-step process in which the patient determines when to face the next item on the list, flooding is immediate. Patients do not control the pace of flooding. Rather, the therapist makes all the decisions.

The idea behind flooding is to place the patient in her most feared situation right away and let her face the symptoms of fear that are so distressing. It is a bit like getting used to the cold water in a swimming pool by diving into the deep end, rather than going in gradually. By facing their worst fears, says therapist Judith Clementson-Mohr, some patients arrive at a surprising conclusion:

There's a notion that if you confront people in a single instance through their worst fear, you flood the emotion of anxiety. They learn from that experience that their fear isn't going to be as destructive as they thought it would be. When they realize that they have lived through it, they lose their irrational fear.[75]

Drawbacks to Behavior Therapy

As effective as they can be, both gradual desensitization and flooding present certain drawbacks. Both methods are time-consuming, because both the therapist and the patient need to visit various sites that induce the fear. The patient needs to directly confront the panic or anxiety, while the therapist provides reassurance that the fear can be managed.

For women with a fear of heights, for instance, an office visit would be virtually useless. To conquer the phobia, both would need to travel to a downtown building, perhaps with a glass elevator, or to the top level of a parking ramp—any location that would provide an opportunity for the patient to experience her phobia.

In addition to being time consuming, such sessions out of the office are often susceptible to interruptions. If the patient was dealing with her fear of stepping into a glass elevator, for example, and there were others around who were impatient to use the elevator, it would be impossible for the patient and therapist to continue with their session.

Cyber Heights and Virtual Snakes?

For this reason, therapy has benefited from virtual reality technology, which uses computers to generate images of bats, spiders, heights, and many other frightening things. Wearing a special head-mounted display that projects images onto two television screens in front of him, the patient also has a position tracker and a sensor that changes his view with even the slightest movement.

"Anyone who's ever experienced virtual reality knows how realistic it is," says one teen who used the method to overcome her fear of snakes. "There's sound, there's color—it's not like watching television. You feel like you're right there. And yeah, it's scary!"[76]

Because virtual reality can put their patients into contact with more phobic situations than they could do themselves, many therapists are finding it a valuable tool. As one researcher says, virtual reality "offers more control and more convenience than the traditional technique. It can take people up in that elevator or out on that parking deck without leaving the therapist's office."[77]

Help for Agoraphobics

Behavioral therapies have helped those with many simple and social phobias for decades, but many of those battling agoraphobia seemed to be less responsive to treatment. The sheer strength of the random panic attack—and the resulting anxiety that it will happen again—often seemed to be no match for desensitization, flooding, and relaxation techniques.

However, many therapists have found that certain medications have the capacity to block such random panic attacks. Two classes of antidepressants—tricyclics and monoamine oxidase (MAO) inhibitors—have been shown to be effective in stopping panic attacks in many patients. Once the threat of a panic attack is minimized, an agoraphobic person can concentrate on dealing with feared situations with behavior therapies.

There are certain side effects to these medications, however, some of them severe. For instance, there are certain foods that interact with the MAO inhibitors such as yogurt, certain kinds of beans, yeast used in brewing beer, chocolate, and other foods with caffeine. When MAO inhibitors and these foods are combined, it

Panic attacks may cause an agoraphobic deep despair. However, therapists are finding that, in some cases, certain drugs can block such attacks.

may result in a dangerous spike in blood pressure. The side effects of tricyclics include blurred vision, dizziness, and excessive sweating.

But by closely monitoring their use, therapists can use these drugs to stop the panic attacks and begin working with their phobic patients on those situations that they've "learned" to avoid. Many therapists, although preferring to cure phobias without medication, see the value in a combination of therapy and antidepressants—and so do their patients.

"Sometimes, I'd open my mouth to say something," remembers one young woman who suffered from panic and a severe social phobia, "and absolutely nothing would come out. It was horrible. Six years of therapy didn't help. But once the medication started to kick in, I stopped having all those frozen moments. I'd been crippled for almost twenty years, and after a couple of weeks on medication, it was over. . . . For the first time in my life, I had some confidence in myself." [78]

"I've Grabbed My Life Back"

Psychologists are very enthusiastic about their success with phobic patients. No longer is it necessary for people to hide from their unreasonable fears and anxiety. The outlook for people with phobias—even for those whose lives have been crippled by agoraphobia—is very bright.

With the help of professionals many phobics overcome their fears and enjoy a normal life.

"Really, my life is full of a lot of 'I wish thats' and 'I wish I hadn't,'" says Anne of her long bout with agoraphobia. "I wasted so much of my life, so much of my kids' lives that I can't get back. But I'm over the worst of it, and I'm so grateful.

"I could never, never have come out of my home without the support of my therapist and my family. Once the panic attacks were controlled, we started using relaxation techniques and behavior therapy to help me learn to get into a car again. I feel like I've grabbed my life back.

"I know that I will sometimes feel anxious, feel nervous . . . but I can deal with it—I've learned how. I am proud of myself for doing battle with this big ugly monster I've been living with, this fear. And I won! I did it!"[79]

Notes

Introduction: The Most Dreadful Feeling

1. Personal interview, Sherri, Bloomington, MN, May 4, 2000.
2. Telephone interview, Greg, April 25, 2000.
3. Telephone interview, Bruce, May 7, 2000.
4. Quoted in L. Wayne Hicks, "Phobia Is No Joke to Employee Paralyzed by an Irrational Fear," *Denver Business Journal*, March 26, 1990, p. 20.
5. Personal interview, Magdeline, Bloomington, MN, May 2, 2000.
6. Quoted in Stephen Perrine, "Phobias: The Facts About Fears," *Parents Magazine*, September 1989, p. 211.

Chapter 1: Fear and Phobia

7. Quoted in Donald W. Goodwin, *Phobia: The Facts*. Oxford, England: Oxford University Press, 1983, p. 2.
8. Isaac M. Marks, *Fears, Phobias, and Rituals: Panic, Anxiety, and Their Disorders*. New York: Oxford University Press, 1987, p. 3.
9. Goodwin, *Phobia*, pp. 2–3.
10. Quoted in Marks, *Fears, Phobias, and Rituals*, p. 3.
11. Telephone interview, Suzy, May 1, 2000.
12. Personal interview, Susan, Minneapolis, MN, May 13, 2000.
13. Telephone interview, Tim, May 3, 2000.
14. Goodwin, *Phobia*, p. 7.
15. Personal interview, Pat, Richfield, MN, April 13, 2000.
16. Personal interview, Gilian, Minneapolis, MN, May 20, 2000.
17. Personal interview, Terri, Edina, MN, May 14, 2000.

Chapter 2: History and Early Research

18. Quoted in Fraser Kent, *Nothing to Fear: Coping with Phobias*. Garden City, NJ: Doubleday, 1977, p. 11.

19. Quoted in Ronald M. Doctor and Ada Kahn, *The Encyclopedia of Phobias, Fears, and Anxieties.* New York: Facts On File, 1989, p. 312.
20. Quoted in Doctor and Kahn, *Encyclopedia,* p. 423.
21. Quoted in Doctor and Kahn, *Encyclopedia,* p. 312.
22. Quoted in Doctor and Kahn, *Encyclopedia,* p. 313.
23. Telephone interview, (name withheld for privacy reasons), May 14, 2000.
24. Kent, *Nothing to Fear,* p. 23.
25. Quoted in Goodwin, *Phobia,* p. 80.
26. Doctor and Kahn, *Encyclopedia,* p. 314.
27. Quoted in Carolyn J. Gard, "Coping with the Fear of Fear," *Current Health 2,* January 1999, p. 22.

Chapter 3: Social and Specific Phobias
28. Telephone interview, Candy, May 28, 2000.
29. Quoted in Amy Sunshine-Genova, "Say Goodbye to Shy," *Cosmopolitan,* October 1991, p. 135.
30. Quoted in Sunshine-Genova, "Say Goodbye to Shy," p. 135.
31. Telephone interview, (name withheld for privacy reasons), May 27, 2000.
32. Quoted in Sunshine-Genova, "Say Goodbye to Shy," p. 134.
33. Murray B. Stein, "How Shy Is Too Shy?" *Lancet,* April 27, 1996, p. 1,132.
34. Jerilyn Ross, *Triumph over Fear: A Book of Help and Hope for People with Anxiety, Panic Attacks, and Phobias.* New York: Bantam Books, 1994, p. 36.
35. Personal interview, Terri, Minneapolis, MN, June 1, 2000.
36. Dennis Beaver, "Got Stage Fright?" *ABA Banking Journal,* February 1998, p. 96.
37. Quoted in Kent, *Nothing to Fear,* p. 67.
38. Quoted in Lesley Jane Seymour, "Fear of Almost Everything," *Mademoiselle,* September 1993, p. 252.
39. Quoted in Toddi Gutner, "High Anxiety," *Forbes,* September 30, 1991, p. 166.
40. Quoted in "Battling Bashful Bladder Syndrome," *USA Today Magazine,* October 1994, p. 13.

41. Quoted in "Battling Bashful Bladder Syndrome," p. 13.
42. Telephone interview, Clare, June 1, 2000.
43. Personal interview, (name withheld for privacy reasons), Richfield, MN, June 7, 2000.

Chapter 4: Simple Phobias

44. Quoted in Stephen Rae, "Who's Afraid of the Big Bad Phobia?" *Cosmopolitan*, September 1994, p. 218.
45. Telephone interview, (name withheld for privacy reasons), May 13, 2000.
46. Telephone interview, (name withheld for privacy reasons), June 1, 2000.
47. Eloise Salholz et al., "The Fight to Conquer Fear," *Newsweek*, April 23, 1984, p. 68.
48. Marks, *Fears, Phobias, and Rituals*, p. 375.
49. Telephone interview, Lorne, May 13, 2000.
50. Marks, *Fears, Phobias, and Rituals*, p. 375.
51. Kent, *Nothing to Fear*, p. 83.
52. Quoted in Marks, *Fears, Phobias, and Rituals*, p. 382.
53. Personal interview, (name withheld for privacy reasons), Edina, MN, May 20, 2000.
54. Personal interview, Rachael, Minneapolis, MN, June 1, 2000.
55. Telephone interview, Terri, June 16, 2000.

Chapter 5: Panic Attacks and Agoraphobia

56. Quoted in Doctor and Kahn, *Encyclopedia*, p. 14.
57. Telephone interview, Anne, June 1, 14, 15, 2000.
58. Salholz, "The Fight to Conquer Fear," p. 69.
59. Katherine Weissman, "The Nightmare of Agoraphobia: A True Tale," *Cosmopolitan*, December 1993, p. 113.
60. Quoted in "When Fear Takes Control," *Teen*, January 1995, p. 25.
61. Telephone interview, Anne.
62. Telephone interview, Anne.
63. Telephone interview, Anne.
64. Personal interview, Anne, Minneapolis, MN, May 13, 2000.
65. Telephone interview, (name withheld for privacy reasons), May 2, 2000.

66. Telephone interview, (name withheld for privacy reasons), May 2, 2000.

67. Telephone interview, Anne.

Chapter 6: Overcoming Phobias

68. Personal interview, Lou, Richfield, MN, May 2, 2000.

69. Quoted in Perrine, "Phobias," p. 20.

70. Quoted in Aurora Mackey, "Your Fears: You Can Overcome Them," *Teen*, February 1983, p. 19.

71. Telephone interview, Lou, June 16, 2000.

72. Goodwin, *Phobia*, p. 105.

73. Quoted in "A Seminar for the Terrified," *Life*, July 1995, p. 28.

74. Quoted in "Battling Bashful Bladder Syndrome," p. 13.

75. Quoted in Mackey, "Your Fears," p. 18.

76. Personal interview, Tara, Bloomington, MN, May 3, 2000.

77. Marty Munson and Teresa Yeykal, "Virtually Fearless," *Prevention*, September 1995, p. 37.

78. Quoted in Sunshine-Genova, "Say Goodbye to Shy," p. 136.

79. Telephone interview, Anne.

For Further Reading

Shirley Babior and Carol Goldman, *Overcoming Panic Anxiety and Phobias*. Duluth, MN: Pfeifer-Hamilton, 1996. Interesting case studies and examples of things that do not help agoraphobics with their fears.

Raeann Dumont, *The Sky Is Falling: Understanding and Coping with Phobias, Panic, and Obsessive-Compulsive Disorders*. New York: W. W. Norton, 1996. Fascinating case studies of people with various phobias.

Lynn Freeman, *Panic Free: Eliminate Anxiety/Panic Attacks Without Drugs and Take Control of Your Life*. Colorado Springs, CO: Health-Wise, 1998. Very current section on medications being used today to treat symptoms of agoraphobia and other anxieties.

Douglas Hunt, *No More Fears: How to Free Yourself from Disabling Phobias and Unreasonable Panic with a Simple, New Program of Nutritional Supplements*. New York: Warner, 1988. Interesting alternatives to counseling and drugs for phobic people; good index.

Janice McLean and Sheila A. Knights, *Phobics and Other Panic Victims*. New York: Continuum, 1989. Excellent annotated bibliography.

Judy Monroe, *Phobias: Everything You Wanted to Know, but Were Afraid to Ask*. Springfield, NJ: Enslow, 1996. Helpful glossary, as well as a fairly inclusive list of various simple phobias.

Karen P. Williams, *How to Help Your Loved One Recover from Agoraphobia*. Far Hills, NJ: New Horizons Press, 1993. Interesting view of the phobia from the family's perspective.

R. Reid Wilson, *Don't Panic: Taking Control of Anxiety Attacks*. New York: Harper, 1996. Intended as a self-help book for people with agoraphobia and social phobias, this gives a very thorough background of the physiological components of fear and panic.

Joseph Wolpe, *Life Without Fear: Anxiety and Its Cure*. Oakland, CA: New Harbinger, 1988. Good section on "flooding" as a method of easing phobias.

Works Consulted

Books

Ronald M. Doctor and Ada Kahn, *The Encyclopedia of Phobias, Fears, and Anxieties.* New York: Facts On File, 1989. Extremely helpful volume; very inclusive and readable for the layperson. Good section on the history of phobia research.

Donald W. Goodwin, *Phobia: The Facts.* Oxford, England: Oxford University Press, 1983. Excellent notes and references; good section on childhood phobias.

Fraser Kent, *Nothing to Fear: Coping with Phobias.* Garden City, NJ: Doubleday, 1977. An older book, but very readable; good material on how people "learn" phobias. Very comprehensive appendix listing medical terms for hundreds of phobias.

Isaac M. Marks, *Fears, Phobias, and Rituals: Panic, Anxiety, and Their Disorders.* New York: Oxford University Press, 1987. Difficult reading, but extremely informative to the reader who can wade through it. Good history of fear research, as well as fascinating case studies of phobic patients.

Jerilyn Ross, *Triumph over Fear: A Book of Help and Hope for People with Anxiety, Panic Attacks, and Phobias.* New York: Bantam Books, 1994. Very engrossing, with an excellent sampling of case studies; good resource list.

Periodicals

Tom Barry, "Curing Phobias: That's Just One Benefit from Start-Up," *Georgia Trend,* November 1998.

"Battling Bashful Bladder Syndrome," *USA Today Magazine,* October 1994.

Jennifer Beauprez, "Phobia Therapy Takes Flight: Psychologist's

88

New Clinic Addresses Airplane Fears," *Crain's Cleveland Business,* November 10, 1997.

Dennis Beaver, "Got Stage Fright?" *ABA Banking Journal,* February 1998.

Susan Chollar, "Fear of Fillings," *Psychology Today,* January/February 1989.

Carolyn J. Gard, "Coping with the Fear of Fear," *Current Health 2,* January 1999.

Toddi Gutner, "High Anxiety," *Forbes,* September 30, 1991.

Lynne Hall, "Fighting Phobias: The Things That Go Bump in the Mind," *FDA Consumer,* March 1997.

L. Wayne Hicks, "Phobia Is No Joke to Employee Paralyzed by an Irrational Fear," *Denver Business Journal,* March 26, 1990.

Bill LeGro, "When Panic Strikes . . . Don't Panic," *Prevention,* April 1989.

Aurora Mackey, "Your Fears: You Can Overcome Them," *Teen,* February 1983.

Marty Munson and Teresa Yeykal, "Virtually Fearless," *Prevention,* September 1995.

Cathy Perlmutter, "5 Who Conquered Fear," *Prevention,* July 1992.

Stephen Perrine, "Phobias: The Facts About Fears," *Parents Magazine,* September 1989.

"Phobias: How They're Caused, How They Can Be Treated," *U.S. News & World Report,* December 17, 1984.

Stephen Rae, "Who's Afraid of the Big Bad Phobia?" *Cosmopolitan,* September 1994.

Eloise Salholz et al., "The Fight to Conquer Fear," *Newsweek,* April 23, 1984.

Joannie M. Schrof, "Why Everyone Gets Stage Fright," *U.S. News & World Report,* June 21, 1999.

"A Seminar for the Terrified," *Life,* July 1995.

Lesley Jane Seymour, "Fear of Almost Everything," *Mademoiselle,* September 1993.

Murray B. Stein, "How Shy Is Too Shy?" *Lancet,* April 27, 1996.

Amy Sunshine-Genova, "Say Goodbye to Shy," *Cosmopolitan,* October 1991.

Katherine Weissman, "The Nightmare of Agoraphobia: A True Tale," *Cosmopolitan,* December 1993.

"When Fear Takes Control," *Teen,* January 1995.

Index

Picture Credits

About the Author

Gail B. Stewart received her undergraduate degree from Gustavus Adolphus College in St. Peter, Minnesota. She did her graduate work in English, linguistics, and curriculum study at the College of St. Thomas and the University of Minnesota. She taught English and reading for more than ten years.

She has written over ninety books for young people, including a series for Lucent Books called The Other America. She has written many books on historical topics such as World War I and the Warsaw ghetto.

Stewart and her husband live in Minneapolis with their three sons, Ted, Elliot, and Flynn; two dogs; and a cat. When she is not writing she enjoys reading, walking, and watching her sons play soccer.